AF349331

SILVIA SÁNCHEZ CALDERÓN

# LEARNING ENGLISH THROUGH ICT TOOLS

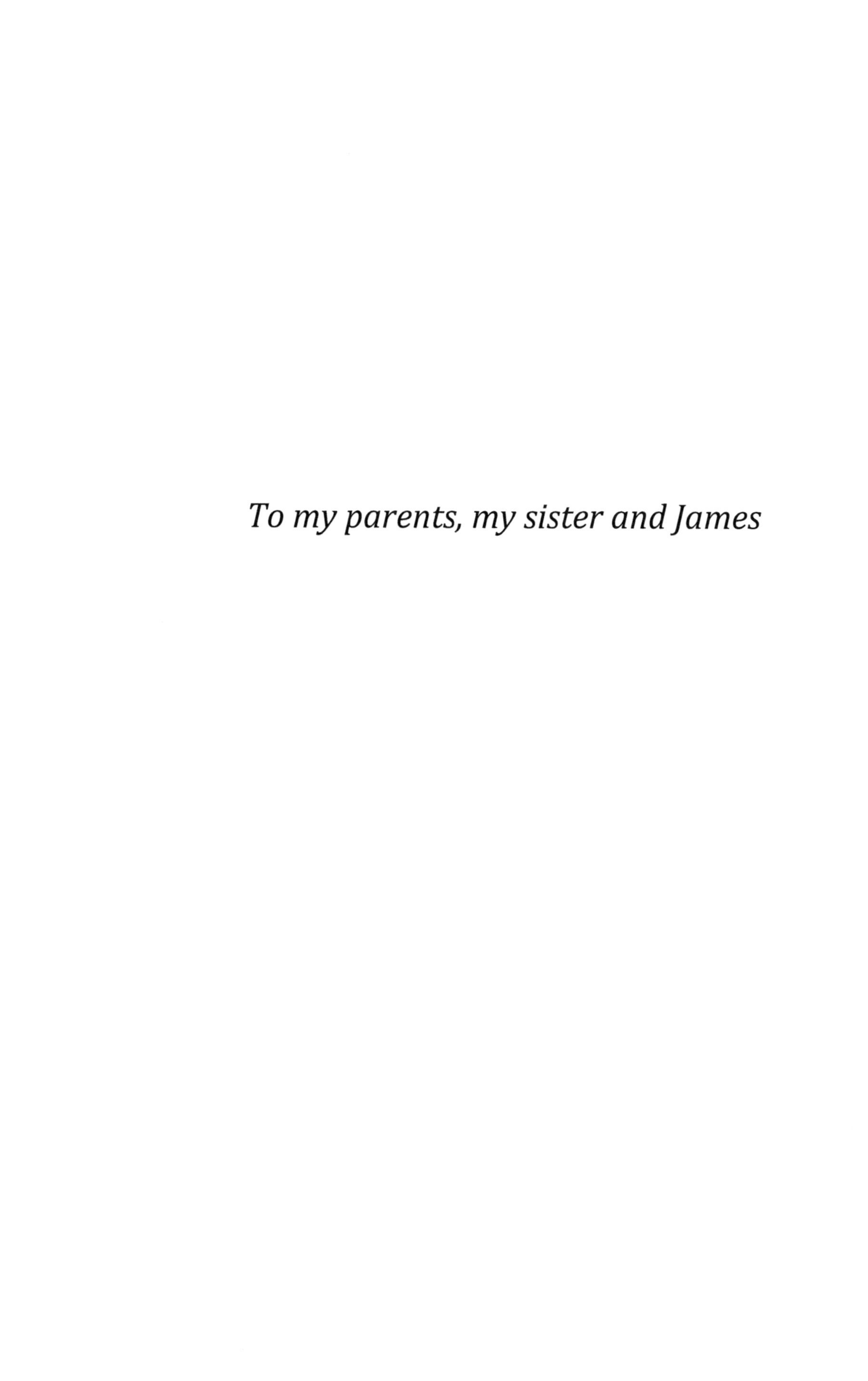

*To my parents, my sister and James*

# Table of contents

# Introduction

The present book has been written for teachers and students of English as a second language (L2, henceforth) and considers the three educational levels, namely, school, college and university. They will find it as a useful resource since it provides readers with insights, suggestions and approaches to implement the so-called Information and Communication Technology (ICT, henceforth) tools to develop the four language skills, namely, reading, writing, listening and speaking, along with a grammar knowledge. More specifically, this book will contribute to help L2 English teachers in designing creative and motivating lesson plans in which L2 English students will learn English through the use of ICT tools while developing several competences such as the digital competence, the learning to learn (that is to say, they learn by doing), autonomy and an active role given they are responsible for their own learning. In this student-centred approach, the teacher is a guide and a facilitator of resources.

The resources described in this book will foster L2 English teachers and L2 English learning to consider that lesson plans are more effective when the teacher has determined the learning and teaching objectives for both ICT and English. A detailed explanation regarding how each ICT tool functions is provided in the corresponding chapters so that L2 English teachers are able to build standing selection criteria when applying each ICT tool in the classroom.

The main features of the book include the following factors that are associated with the role played by ICT tools in teaching and learning English as an L2:

a) A general overview of ICT and its impact on education (chapter 1)
b) ICT tools to be implemented in the teaching and in the learning practices (chapter 2)
c) The use of the Internet and the potential online resources available for educational purposes (chapter 3)
d) The implementation of ICT tools to enhance communication and collaborative work (chapter 4)

Chapter 1 offers background information regarding ICT tools (definition and main applications) and its relation to education and the curriculum. A historical development of the role played by ICT in educational settings is also discussed.

Chapter 2 includes the main contributions of ICT tools in the L2 English teaching and learning practice. More specifically, it presents effective tools to foster interpersonal communication and those ones that involve searching and analyzing information. It provides useful insights to working with videos such as YouTube or ESL video to motivate students in the L2 English learning process. For example, teachers will learn how to create and edit dubbed videos as well as finding audiovisual resources organized into language levels. Other multimedia resources will be discussed such as infographics to develop the L2 English students' literacy skills.

Chapter 3 focuses on the historical background of the Internet and the licenses of use that users should be considered before using a resource that is available on the Internet, namely, copyright and open licenses such as creative commons or copyleft. This chapter also presents the ins and outs and the educational applications of the electronic email, the distribution lists, scientific information retrieval, dictionaries and translation programs and using ICT to analyze language via corpus. Furthermore, it provides insights into online teaching resources such as the design of an imaginary Facebook page via ClassTools to develop the English writing skills or creating and using previously available podcasts to enhance the English listening comprehension skills.

Chapter 4 explores the main features and the educational use of the so-called web 2.0 that enables L2 English teachers and learners to communicate with other users through ICT tools such as blogs, Dropbox, Flickr, social networks and wikis, among others.

# Chapter 1

# ICT and its impact on education: History and development

## 1. ICT: DEFINITION AND APPLICATIONS

ICT stands for Information and Communication Technology (Ambròs Pallares and Breu Pañella 2007; Anderson and Van Weert 2002; Area 2009; among others). It is defined as the combination of information technology (IT) with other, related technologies, specifically communication technology (Toledo Morales and Hervas Gómez 2009; Vivancos 2008). ICT is used, applied and integrated in activities of working and learning based on IT methods.

Furthermore, ICT implies tasks related to accessing information on the Internet, storing, manipulating, exchanging and retrieving information from datasets, spreadsheets and in other related forms such as processed sheets or computer-designed images, audio or video (Barba Coromines et al. 2010; Barberá 2004; Ruiz Dávila et al. 2010). Therefore, ICT tools allow to present information in a wide range of ways, namely, animated diagrams, images, speech, sound clips, text and videoclips.

ICT presents some disadvantages regarding the frequency with which new tools and new resources are developed and the speed with which they are updated. Nevertheless, ICT provides with great potential in educational contexts, namely, colleges, schools and universities. This triggers educational institutions to adapt and change the students and the teachers' needs and expectations.

ICT tools allow teachers and students to interact and collaborate with a wide range of peers, regardless of their geographical location. However, the use of ICT tools will require users to develop certain skills in order to search for, analyze, evaluate and present information successfully (Bennett 2004; Bernat and Gros 2008). Examples of ICT tools include the MERLOT (Multimedia Educational Resource for Learning and Online Teaching) system that provides online access to learning resources and content creation tools, as available in www.merlot.org/merlot. This system has been led by an international community of teachers, learners and researchers.

The generations that were born with the Internet and ICT tools have been known as Digital Natives, Gamer Generation, Google generation, Homo Zappiens generation, Messenger generation or New Millenum Learners (Blanco and Cervera 2010; Cabero Almenara 2006, 2007). Indeed, the Internet and ICT tools enable users to navigate through the information available via the use of hyperlinks.

Why should we make use of ICT? One of the answers involves learning from others. Furthermore, it allows to work collaboratively in constructing learning, share teaching experiences and follow another teacher's work. Moreover, it provides learners with a stable background, resources and tools as well as it creates meaningful learning contexts. ICT also guarantees fast access to knowledge and knowledge exchange. This will require users to have developed the so-called information competence, namely, the capacity of knowing how to access, select and restructure information (Silva Salinas 2005; Souto Moure 2006; Temprano Sánchez 2011).

Further positive effects on the role played by ICT in learning are listed below (Cabero Almenara and Román Graván 2008; Segovia García 2006; Sevillano García and Fernández Muñoz 2002):

- Allowance of constant repetition of the same task until the learner has developed the skill via self-correction
- Collaborative work and collaborative learning that allows to edit documents collaboratively (for instance, via Google Drive available in https://www.google.com/drive/) as well as to store and share information, documents and decisions with other users (for example, via Dropbox available in www.dropbox.com). Recall that, on Dropbox, we can retrieve deleted documents and files from the history although it is restricted to a period of 30 days. Only the paid version of Dropbox offers unlimited access to the Dropbox history
- Communication with peers and teachers in national and in international contexts
- Development of autonomy and learning independence
- Enhancement of motivation and enjoyment
- Fostering of inter-personal communication by means of audios, emails, forums, interactive whiteboards and videoconferences, among others

- Improvement of academic performance (that is, increase of concentration and time spent on tasks)
- Keeping students updated
- Learning at the students' pace
- Quick feedback and assessment
- Storage of information
- Student-centered approach, namely, students are the main characters in the learning/teaching practice. Teachers will play a crucial role in the educational program since they will be facilitators of the students' learning
- Teachers' management of students' group works

Recently, educational tasks have been influenced using computers, multimedia tools and the Internet. Teachers are required to be encouraged in new ICT advances and, thus, incorporated them in their lesson plans in their daily teaching practices. From the students' perspective, although they are Digital Natives, they also need to be frequently updated and prepared for changes that the learning process requires.

E-learning began in 2000 from the Commission of the European Communities in Lisbon. The Commission of the European Communities (2001) stated that e-learning is the education of the future. It involves any form of learning and teaching that is mainly supported by the implementation of new ICT tools and, more specifically, the use of the Internet. In addition, the Commission of the European Communities (2001) guaranteed that the countries that constitute the European Union will be provided with Internet access by 2001 in all the European schools along with a transeuropean network to ensure communication among colleges, research centers, scientific libraries, schools and universities, among others. Therefore, e-learning aims to:

- Develop high quality contents and services
- Establish new forms of teacher-student communication via the use of ICT tools
- Interconnect spaces and virtual platforms to favor the process of teaching and distance education as a complementary resource of the traditional face-to-face teaching practice
- Provide institutions with education, knowledge and training

The European Computer Driving License (ECDL) is the world's ICT skill certification (see further information in http://ecdl.org/). In other words, it is an international certificate that is acknowledged worldwide to prove basic knowledge and the necessary skills required to use computers by means of the use of the most common applications. ECDL is supervised by Accredited Test Centers (ATCs). Figure 1 shows the countries where ECDL is acknowledged.

Figure 1. Countries where ECDL is acknowledged (ECDL guide: 4)

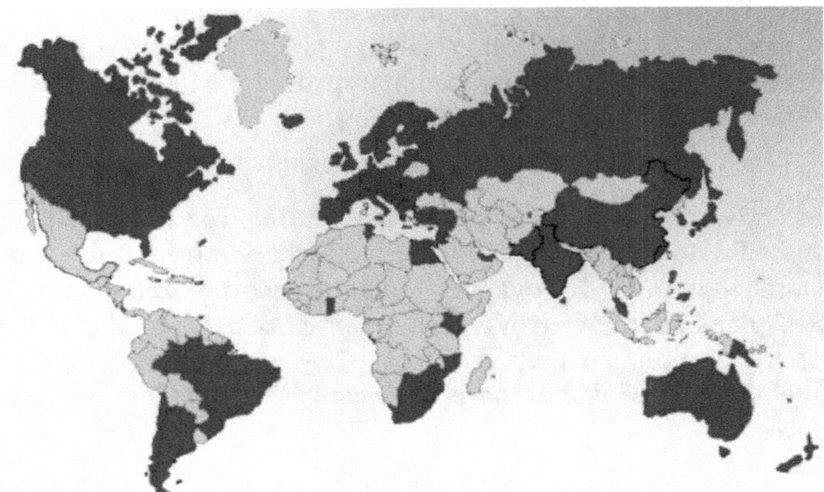

ECDL is a test that includes theoretical questions (basic IT concepts) and practical questions (use of common applications in computers). The certificate contributes to widespread the working possibilities and increases the workers' efficiency.

The institutions that acknowledge the ECDL are listed below:

- Education Ministries of Austria, Holland, Hungary, Italy and Poland
- In Spain: The Ministry of Industry, Andalusian Council, Murcia Council, Huesca Town Hall, La Rioja Public Health System and the Local Administration of Badajoz
- Organization for Economic Co-operation and Development (OECD)
- The European Commission
- World Bank

The exam syllabus detailed in hppt://ecdl.ati.es/. There are three level-types of exams, namely, ECDL basic level, ECDL standard level and ECDL advanced. The ECDL basic level exam is required to be passed first before moving on to the advanced level and includes four modules: (a) basic IT knowledge; (b) word processor; (c) excel; and (d) basic knowledge of the Internet. The ECDL standard level exam involves four further modules: (a) presentations; (b) database; (c) IT safety; and (d) online collaboration. The ECDL advanced level exam implies four further modules: (a) word processor; (b) excel; (c) presentation; and (d) databases.

ICT tools facilitate both synchronic and asynchronic communication (Castañeda Quintero 2010; Castro Sánchez 2004; Cervera and Blanco 2010; Gallego and Gatica 2006). In online learning, synchronic communication means group work live by means of audioconferences, chats, interactive whiteboards and videoconferences. In chat rooms, users comment to each other's real-time discussions. Likewise, audio and videoconferences favor real-time communication as it occurs online. Therefore, learning from synchronous ICT communication tools fosters users to verbalize their thoughts and retain concepts and information more effectively.

An example of a synchronous communication tool is the whiteboard Notebook Cast available in https://www.notebookcast.com/es/board/open/new. Figure 2 illustrates the writing and editing tools available in the whiteboard.

Figure 2. Writing and editing tools in Spanish for Notebook Case

*Lápiz* = pencil. *Deshacer* = remove. *Borrador* = rubber. *Papel* = paper.

Figure 3 shows the types of line styles (namely, thin, medium and thick) in writing as well as a wide range of shapes (namely, line, square and circle) to be included in the whiteboard.

Figure 3. Types of line in writing and shapes in Spanish for Notebook Case

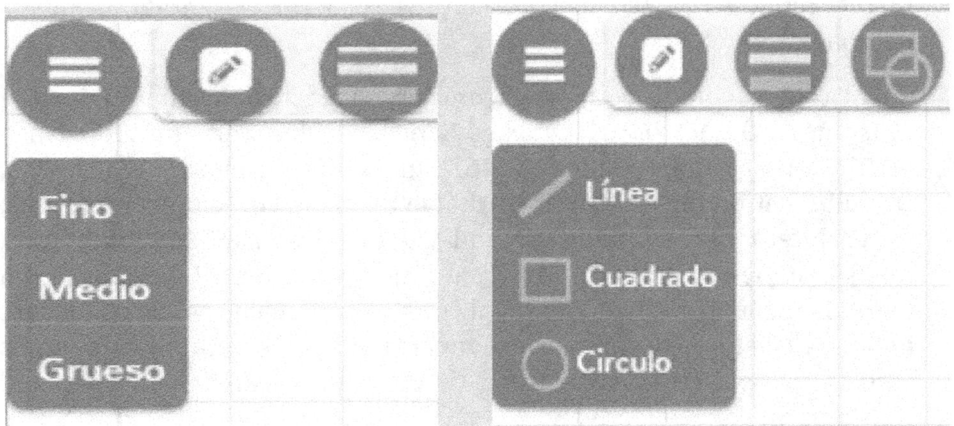


*Fino* = thin. *Medio* = médium. *Grueso* = thick. *Línea* = line. *Cuadrado* = square. *Círculo* = circle

Figure 4 illustrates the varied color palette to be incorporated in the whiteboard Notebook Case.

Figure 4. Color palette in Notebook Case

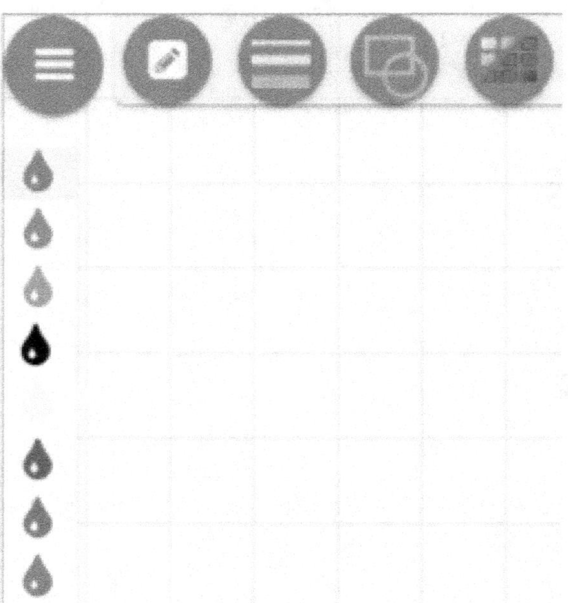

By contrast, asynchronous communication implies a time lag via blogs, calendars, distribution lists, emails, forums, wikis. The time lag in communication aids users to process information and develop their own thoughts on the issues discussed given that they have more time to explore ideas or, simply, more time for considering what they are going to discuss. One of the disadvantages of asynchronous communication is the time delayed when waiting for a response.

Further details of synchronous and asynchronous tools will be discussed in chapter 2 (ICT teaching and learning tools) and in chapter 3 (the Internet and educational resources).

## 2. ICT IN EDUCATION: HISTORICAL DEVELOPMENT

ICT tools emerged with the need to train American soldiers to survive and to perform efficiently in the Second World War (1939-1945) (Castañeda Quintero 2010; De la Cruz Cabanillas and Tejedor Martínez 2003; Fonoll et al. 2011). Hence, several institutions were founded to design movies and other related teaching and learning resources, namely, the Division of Visual Aids for War Training, the Office of Education Training Films and the United States Armed Forces Institute. Gradually, this led schools to adapt the resources designed by the above-mentioned institutions and implemented the use of (non-)silent movies, overhead projects and slides so that they could display efficiency in motivating students while learning as well as in the teaching practices.

A historical overview of the evolution from traditional resources to ICT tools is summarized below (García Valcárcel Muñoz-Repiso and Hernández Martín 2013; Sánchez Rodríguez et al. 2009):

- In 1969, Leonard Kleinrock manages to connect two computers
- In 1972, the email is created
- In 1983, the Internet Protocol (IP) of communication appears. The IP is the identification of the computer and allows to connect networks. It consists of 12 numbers divided into groups of 3 numbers (for instance, 130.206.130.120)
- In 1992, the World Wide Web (www) is created by Robert Cailliau I Tim Berners-Lee. The www allows the design and the distribution of hypertexts that include the following resources: animations, images, sounds, texts and the management of different Internet services such as email files, transfer, among others
- In 1995, the Internet appears

- In the twenty-first century, there is a gradual development of digital literacy, that is to say, teaching involves innovation with the implementation of new ICT resources such as DVDs, online libraries, videoconferences. Furthermore, using ICT tools allows to access information through the use of resources available on the Internet, carry out academic work and conduct research, as well as share and publish information.

A contrast between the traditional learning settings and new learning settings is displayed in Table 1.

Table 1. Traditional and new learning settings

| Traditional learning settings | New learning settings |
|---|---|
| Instruction focused on the teacher | Learning focused on the student |
| One means of communication | Multiple (multimedia) means of communication |
| Individual learning | Cooperative learning |
| Transfer of information | Exchange of information |
| Passive learning | Active or exploratory learning |
| Learning based on facts | Critical learning |
| Isolated and artificial learning background | Authentic and real learning background |

Focusing on the new learning settings in Table 1, ICT influences the teaching practice structure and the relation established between the teacher and the student when compared to the traditional learning settings.

## 3. ICT IN THE CURRICULUM

Escudero (1995) argues that the implementation of ICT tools in the curriculum involves a project to structure the teaching and the learning practices to decide on when, how and why to use ICT tools. The project is required to follow certain criteria, values, students' interests and curriculum objectives.

Nevertheless, ICT tools offer certain disadvantages when implemented the curriculum (Cobo Romaní and Pardo Kuklinski 2007; Cukierman et al. 2009). For example, the use of outdated equipment, the high cost of the tools, the teachers' lack or reduced knowledge and the space adjustments in the educational settings.

Teachers are learning facilitators given that they are responsible for searching for resources for students to access information. Moreover, teachers foster the realization of problem-solving tasks by means of collaborative work. Nevertheless, tele-working and tele-training can be associated with isolation if teachers do not have the capacity of taking advantage of virtual communication settings. In turn, teachers implement a constructive methodological approach and design resources by using ICT tools, diagnose students' academic interests and needs and provide feedback.

Students experience self-learning and self-discipline, as triggered by their active and independent learning roles. Using ICT tools allow students to develop skills related to analysis and synthesis, problem-solving, learning to learn, planning and managing time and information, adjustment to new settings and creativity. Knowledge is exchanged through collaborative work and critical thinking is developed by expressing justified ideas and apply innovative proposals to problem-solving tasks. Overall, students adopt positive attitudes towards ICT tools when compared to traditional learning approaches.

What is the best ICT resource? The main idea is the elaboration of resources that will meet students' needs and interests. Teachers usually design resources based on their prior experience and the choice will depend on the learning objectives, the students' level, the teaching strategies, the technical features, the physical settings, the quality, the availability, the cost, the knowledge and the complexity (Díaz de Prado and Cervera 2010; Escudero 1995). Although there is not a unique effective ICT resource, students and teachers should be familiar with the content provided and be adequate to meet the teaching and the learning objectives. Therefore, resources should not be selected based on the teacher's personal preferences. Decisions about ICT resources should answer three questions: what to teach, how to teach and how to assess.

The following selection factors should be considered by teachers when deciding what the most effective ICT resource is (Gimeno Sanz 2002; Martínez Sánchez and Prendes Espinosa 2008):

- The students' features: age, level, cognitive skills, learning pace, learning strategies, prior knowledge, training
- The teachers' features: training, teaching experience, motivation and attitude towards ICT

- Dimensions of the curriculum: teaching model, aims, content, strategies, teaching approach, tasks
- Physical background: light, sound, setting, availability
- Technical background: flexibility, interaction, complexity, adjustment to learners
- Justified use: objective, efficiency
- Other aspects: cost

In contrast to most curriculum modules, ICT is not only taught in isolated ICT lessons. Rather, it is integrated across all areas of the curriculum in primary, secondary and tertiary education. In the case of the primary school curriculum, students are required to use ICT in 5 or 6 school areas in the IT room.

Barberà and Badia (2004) claim 11 objectives concerning the integration of ICT tools in education:

- Analysis requires observing, analyzing and comparing the data obtained from ICT tools. It also includes asking exploratory questions regarding the process and the partial findings that are being obtained
- Assessment includes the summative evaluation in the implementation of ICT tools
- Communicative given that ICT offers effective communicative contexts. Audience is not surreal since the content of the communication can reach addresses and receive a response in a short time span
- Informative to search for information from different sources that fosters the development of new strategies
- Innovation entails the inclusion a wide range of ICT tools and requires learners to be frequently updated with new ICT devices and resources
- Motivation involves the exploration of new knowledge based on personal paths. Learning focuses on students who decide what to analyze and investigate via ICT tools. Teachers elaborate lesson plans oriented to the students' interests
- Organization proceeds with the teaching and learning practice. For example, the use of files and folders
- Research skills are developed through the assumption of scientific processes to achieve individual or group work

- Responsibility in students' commitment in their own learning to learn
- Socialization includes students in the ICT society and prevents them from digital exclusion
- Training is enhanced via constructive collaborative learning guided by teachers that provide feedback. Students build knowledge so that they can be more actively involved in the learning process. This approach contrasts traditional teaching methods in which knowledge learning is transmitted by the teacher and stored by the students.

Bennett (2004) argues four views on the role played by ICT tools in the educational settings:

- ICT as a foundation subject. ICT should be studied on its own so as to develop skills related to the functioning of a computer as well as a set of specific concepts such as copying, pasting, saving and printing:
- ICT as a learning tool. This involves finding information using a CD-ROM and the Internet, along with sharing and publishing online information
- ICT as a teacher. The teacher offers tasks that meet students' needs, namely, learning how to punctuate a sentence or a spelling practice. These tasks are displayed in a computer program
- ICT as a teaching and administrative aid for teachers. ICT is used to show information and present ideas to students in an appealing way, register and analyze students' progress and design worksheets and access resources for teaching enhancement

In the case of English learning, there are several factors that affect the use of ICT tools in teaching L2 English (Día de Prado and Cervera 2010; Manning et al. 2008):

- Child-related issues: experience, needs, learning styles, behavior
- Personal issues: personality, confidence, experience, attitudes, beliefs
- Relationship issues: child-teacher, teacher-teacher, parent-teacher
- Subject-related issues. For instance, speech acts, sentence structure or spelling

The Spanish Ministry of Education has defined the basic competences established in the Royal Decree 1513/2006, 7 December (in Primary

Education) and 1631/2006, 29 December (in Secondary Education). These competences aim to develop the achievement of personal realization as human beings, active citizenship, become successful adults and be able to develop lifelong learning. ICT is one of the eight educational competences, as established by the OECD throughout the Definition and Selection of Key Competences (DeSeCo) project, as listed below:

1. Communication in your mother tongue
2. Communication in a second language
3. Mathematical competence and basic competence in science and technology
4. Digital competence
5. Learning to learn
6. Interpersonal, intercultural, social and civic competences
7. Entrepeneur spirit
8. Cultural expression

The digital competence consists of skills related to searching, selecting, obtaining, processing, communication, transformation of knowledge and usage. It also requires the knowledge of specific language such as texts, numbers, images and sounds. The digital competence uses several techniques to access information according to the source (namely, audiovisual, bibliographical and oral) and the support (digital, multimedia and printed).

# Chapter 2

# ICT teaching and learning tools

## 1. MAIN CONTRIBUTIONS

This section presents a wide range of ICT tools for teaching and learning English as an L2. More specifically, it focuses on tools that will help in the development of listening comprehension, speaking skills, written production, reading comprehension and grammar.

One of the tools that foster the improvement of L2 English listening comprehension is YouTube. As depicted in Figure 5, YouTube allows to add subtitles that can be added by the video creator who can edit the subtitles in the target language of the video or as translations in the user's first language (L1) (see the *subtítulos* option in Figure 5). Furthermore, the user can auto-generate subtitles in several languages (English, Spanish, French). However, subtitle auto-generation may display wrong words and, in many cases, without the presence of punctuation.

Figure 5. YouTube settings

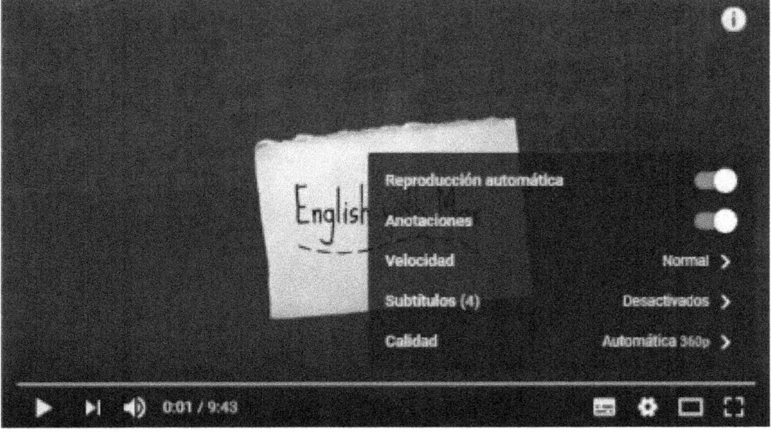

As seen in the option *velocidad* on the Spanish YouTube in Figure 5, L2 English learners can also change the speed of the video, namely, normal, faster (1.25-2.00) or slower (0.25-0.75).

Google video is a google search engine that also allows to access videos. Figure 6 illustrates some examples of videos for learning English.

Figure 6. Google video

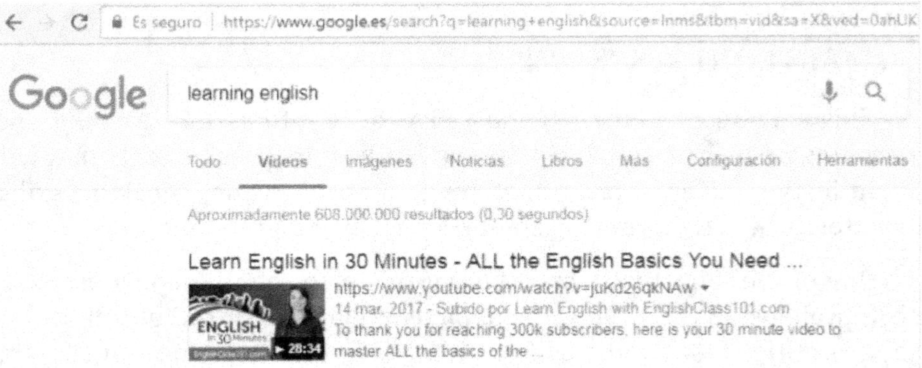

DotSub is a non-free platform that enables uploading our own videos available in https://dotsub.com. Similar to YouTube, subtitles can be added by using as many languages as desired. Figure 7 shows the varied options for hosting videos (for instance, y videos, most viewed, organized in terms of genre or language)

Figure 7. DotSub

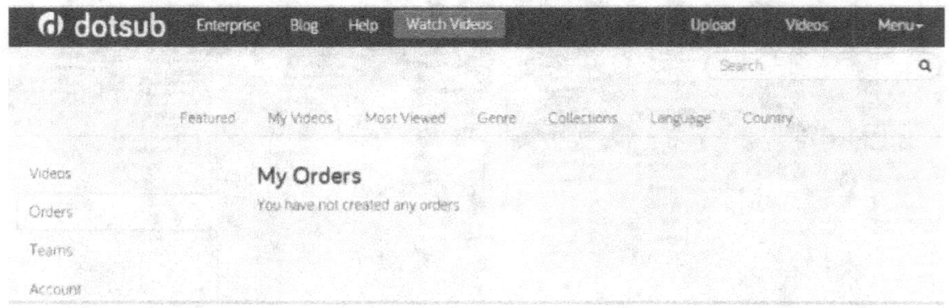

English Central makes a distinction of videos per level. Subtitles can also be added by clicking on the "cc" option once the video is displayed. Figure 8 illustrates L2 English learning videos to learn grammar at intermediate levels. English Central is available in https://es.englishcentral.com/videos.

Figure 8. English Central videos

Regarding the development of speaking skills, Skype (available in https://www.skype.com/es) is a non-online ICT tool that requires to be downloaded. An account is needed so as to add users. It has different functions, namely, free (video-)calls, chat, share documents or images. While (video-)calls are free for skype users (up to 25 people), they are not free to mobile phones and landlines. Users can share their screen while talking. An example of the main skype sign-in page is shown in Figure 9.

Figure 9. Skype

Gtalk (also known as Google Hangouts) allows to make (video-)calls and send text messages. As illustrated in Figure 10, a Gmail registration is needed and up to 10 Gmail account users can be added so as the (video-)calls take place.

Figure 10. Google Hangouts

Gtalk or Google Hangouts can be accessed via Gmail apps (namely, https://hangouts.google.com/hl=es) or, as shown in Figure 11, access can also be done by dragging the corresponding icon.

Figure 11. Gtalk/Google Hangouts

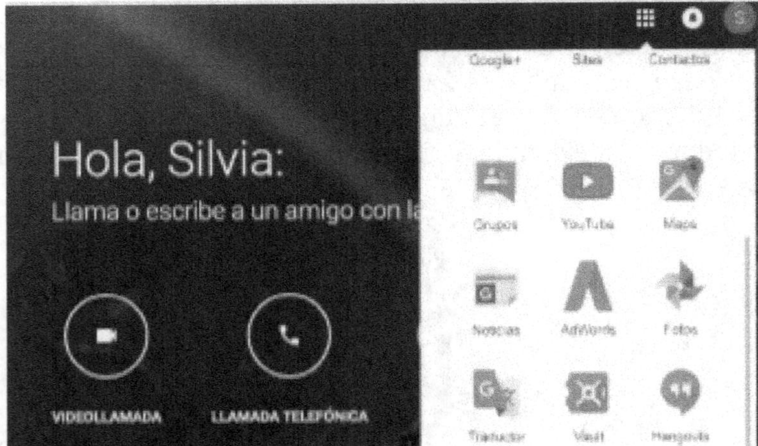

Contacts can be added by typing the Gmail account in and sending an invitation, as shown in Figure 12.

   

Figure 12. Adding contacts in Gtalk/Google Hangouts

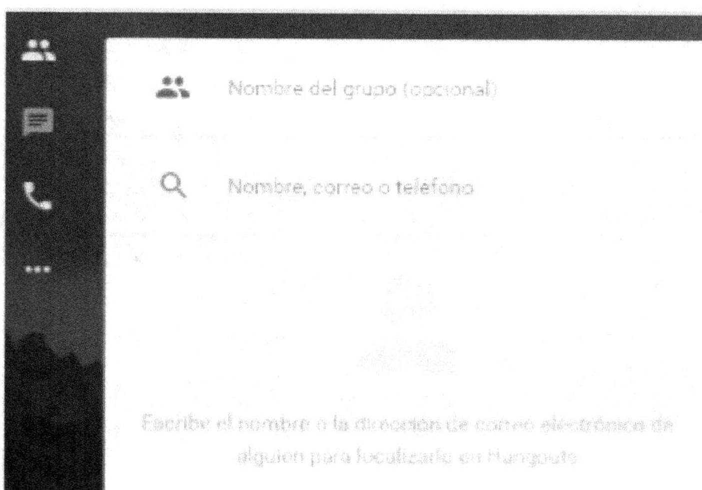

When accessing Gtalk/Google Hangouts, there is a pencil to draw and write. Furthermore, the image icon is used to upload images. These two options are depicted in Figure 13.

Figure 13. Gtalk/Google Hangouts

Sharing screen is also allowed via Gtalk or Google Hangouts. As shown in Figure 14, you can share "all your screen" if you want users to see everything you are doing with your computer while sharing the screen (see the option *toda tu pantalla*) or "a window" if you want users to focus on just one window while you do other things with the computer (see the option *una ventana*).

Figure 14. Sharing screen via Google Hangouts

Why shall we use Gtalk or Google Hangouts in the classroom? One of the answers is that it allows small group collaboration work. Also, live interactive presentations and live broadcast YouTube on your YouTube channel can be displayed. The computer screen can be used for explanations or for power point presentations and, in turn, you can share documents uploaded on Google Drive so that users can edit the document once it has been shared.

As for the improvement of L2 English speaking skills, Gtalk or Google Hangouts allows the access to live broadcast YouTube. In other words, you can log in YouTube with your Gmail account and access My channel on YouTube by clicking on Creator Studio, as depicted in Figure 15.

Figure 15. YouTube channel and Creator Studio

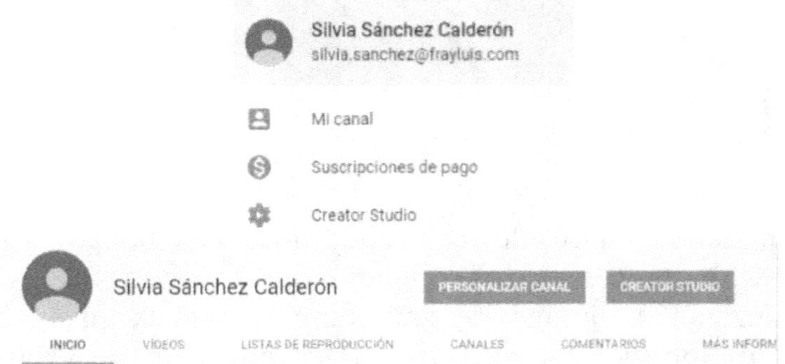

A live stream video or an event can be scheduled or be recorded live by clicking on events (or *eventos*) and new live event (or *nuevo evento en directo*). These two options are shown in Figure 16.

Figure 16. Creating events on My YouTube Channel

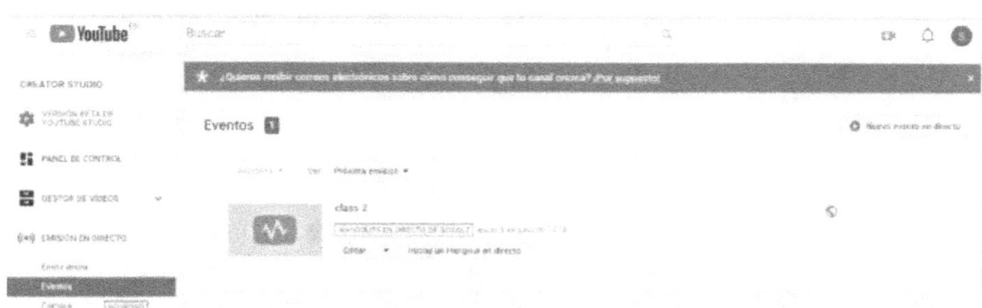

Once the event has been created, a title should be given, a schedule should be arranged (if the event is not live). Moreover, a description of the event and tags or keywords for users to find your videos should be added. The event can be made public, hidden or private. Then, click on "live broadcast" (or *emitir en directo ahora*). These options are shown in Figure 17.

Figure 17. Creating a new event on YouTube

When broadcasting the live YouTube event, it leads to Google Hangouts and, therefore, you can add users or record yourself. As displayed in Figure 18, there is a chat and you can share your screen. In addition, the cameraman allows to mute users or show your users' videos. When you finish, stop broadcasting and hang up.

Figure 18. Live broadcast YouTube settings

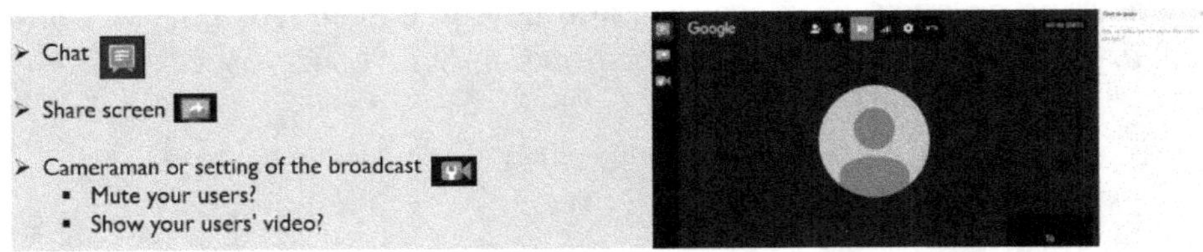


The live broadcast YouTube event can be edited on your YouTube Channel by accessing the video option. Thus, the video can include automatic translations, the URL can be copied to share the video, the front personalized image can be edited, audios already provided by YouTube can be attached to the video, the video can be improved by cutting some parts or by inserting light effects. Subtitles can be added in the speaker's L1 or in a different translated language.

Epals (www.epals.com) is an exchange online program that allows the connection and collaboration among schools for language age-matched communication exchanges. Searches for epals are based on students' interests, school level and language(s) spoken. Epals homepage is shown in Figure 19.

Figure 19. Epals homepage

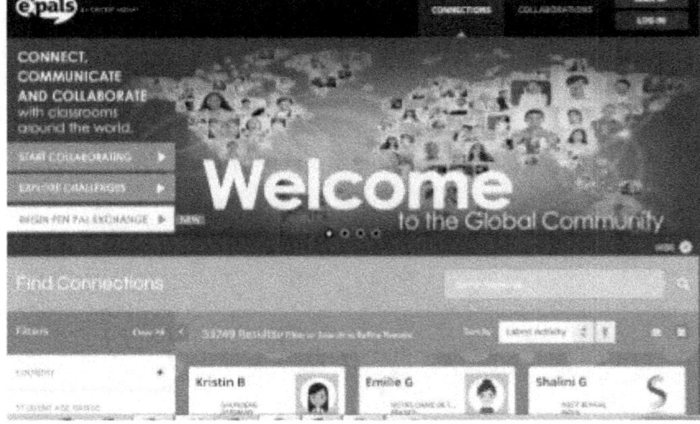


Online text-to-speech programs such as Natural Readers (https://www.naturalreaders.com/online) in Figure 20 or From Text to Speech (http://www.fromtexttospeech.com) in Figure 21 allow to convert a written text into oral speech.

Figure 20. Natural Readers

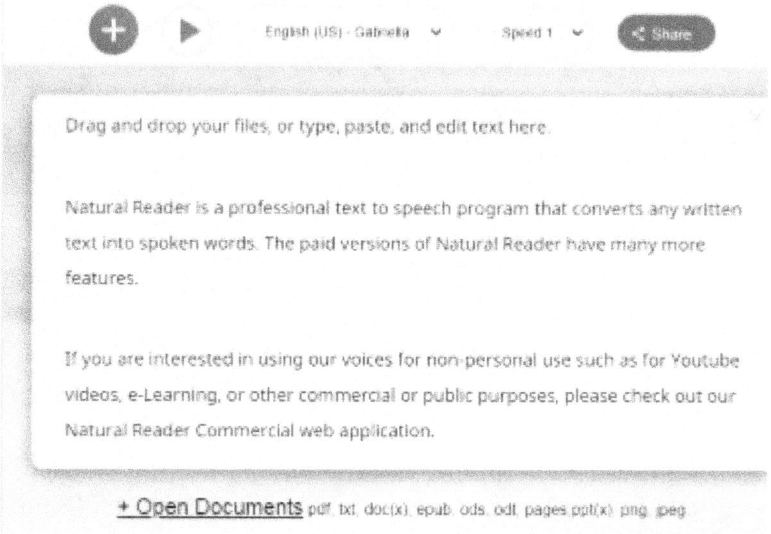

Figure 21. From Text to Speech

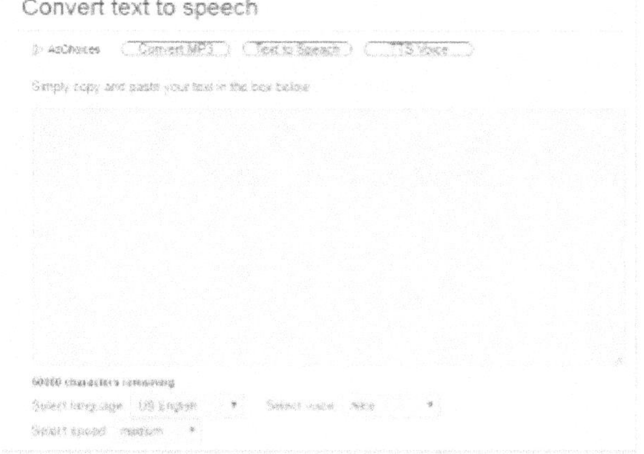

As depicted in Figure 22, Breaking News English, available in https://breakingnewsenglish.com/ enhances the reading comprehension skills along with speaking comprehension and fluency. Users can choose a level, then choose a topic and, finally, click on read. Audio-recordings and their corresponding activities are available in html format so that they can be displayed on the Internet. We can print the activities, listen to them in mp3 and play games related to the podcast. In addition, we can subscribe via RSS to their podcasts and, therefore, we can be informed of updated audio publications.

Figure 22. Breaking News English

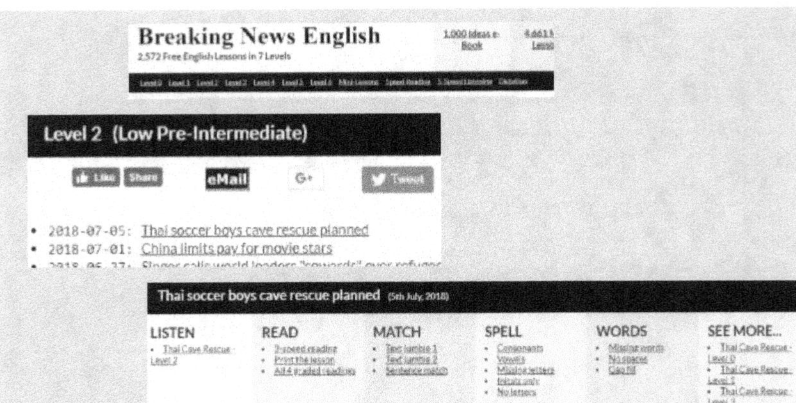

In the case of the development of L2 English writing skills, blogs are an effective ICT tool. As depicted in Figure 23, the British Council bogs hosts English language learning resources available in http://www.teachingenglish.org.uk/blog.

Figure 23. British Council blog

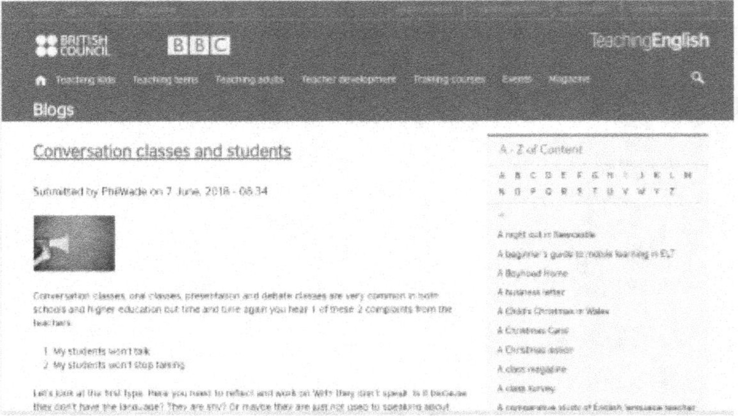

Other ICT tools for L2 English learning include (a) digital books such as the ones available in https://www.digitalbook.io/blog/free-ebooks-for-english-learners/; (b) wikis such as Wikipedia; (c) email addresses that children can correspond with such as "Email Santa" available in https://www.emailsanta.com/; and (d) platforms for the publication of children's written work such as Kidpub available in https://www.kidpub.com.

In the case of the development of English grammar, teachers can create students' tasks via the so-called Web 2.0 programs. Two main programs will be discussed, namely, JClic and HotPotatoes.

JClic was designed by the Department of Education at the University of Barcelona. It was created to support the use of resources created with the free software JClic that allows the creation of several multimedia teaching activities. It requires to be downloaded from http://clil.xtec.cat/es/jclic/index.thm. Java and Java Media Networks need to be installed (see http://clic.xtec.cat/es/jclic/instjava.htm#windows). The resources designed by JClic have a Creative Commons license, which means that the author of these resources allows other users to freely share, use and build upon a work they have elaborated. JClic allows to create crosswords, association exercises or jigsaws. It also enables users to download tasks and save them on the Project library of the computer. Recall that the library is created once JClic is started.

Three programs are installed, namely, JClic displays the created tasks, JClic Author allows to create the tasks and JClic Reports saves the tasks created. For example, if we aim to design an activity based on English countable nouns via JClic Author, Figure 24 shows that, first of all, we access a new project (file (*archivo*) > new project (*new project*)), we give it a title (for instance, countable nouns) and we include the description of the task, the authors' names and the L2 English level.

Figure 24. Creating a new project in JClic Author

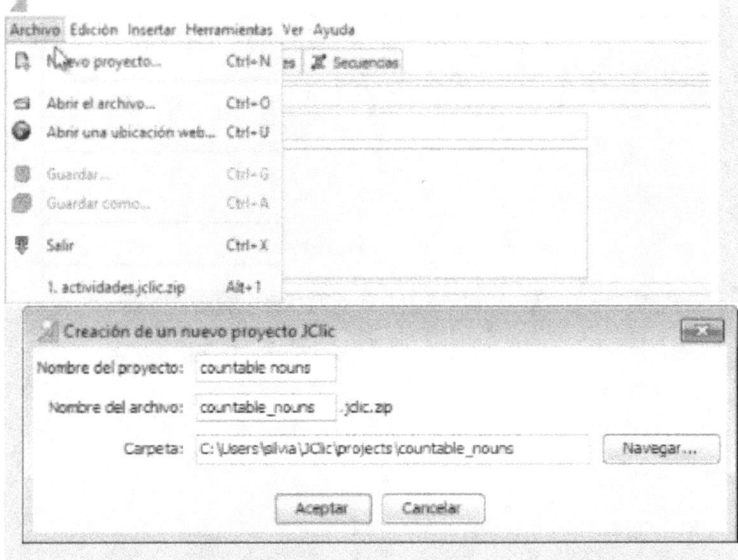

JClic Author's tools include the so-called *Mediateca* that is used to save all the multimedia resources such as audios or images and the type of activities (for instance, complex and simple associations, memory game, exploration, identification, information screen, puzzle, fill in the gaps, identification of elements, order elements, crosswords, and word searches). Figure 25 shows the icon that allows to create a new activity.

Figure 25. Adding a new activity in JClic Author

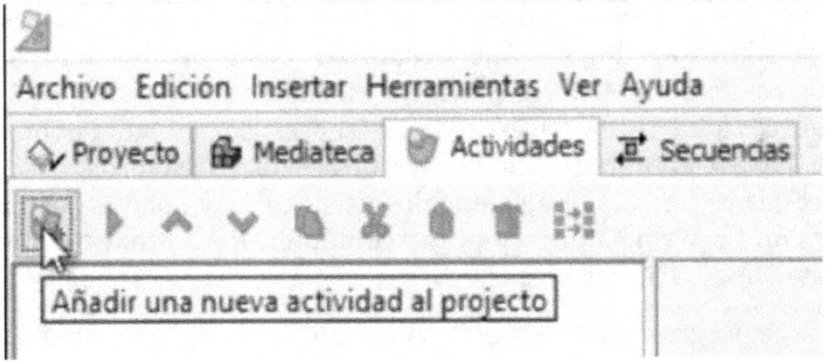

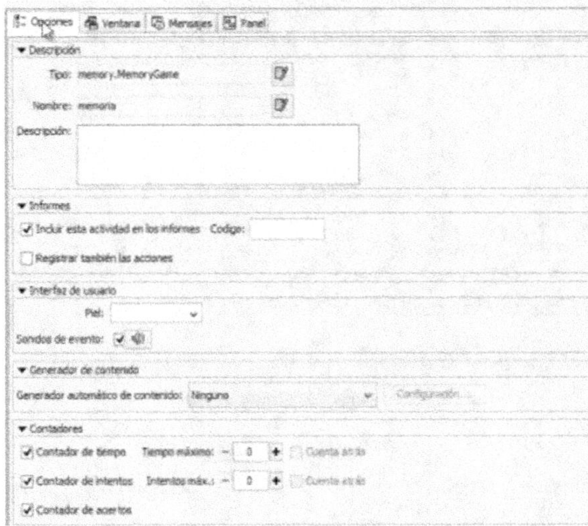


Once the activity to be created has been decided, several options should be considered. As illustrated in Figure 26, the activities should be given a color (see *piel*); sound can be included in the activities (see *sonido del evento*); time should be given to do the activity (see *contador de tiempo*); chances to answer the activity should be set (see *contador de intentos*) and the number of right and wrong answers should be established (see *Contador de aciertos*).

Figure 26. Options in JClic Author

In the window *ventana*, we can personalize the interface of the activities, As depicted in Figure 27, we can design the background color and the image, among others.

Figure 27. Window option in JClic Author

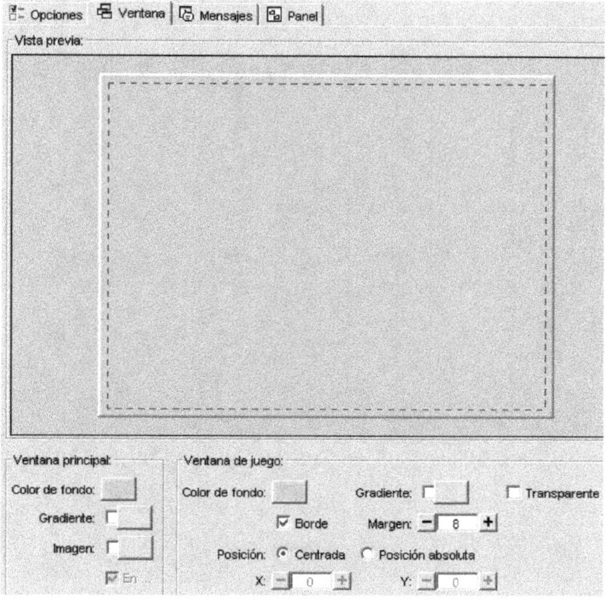

Messages can be included in JClic Author as an introductory message (see Figure 28) or as an edited or retrial message (e.g. please try again).

Figure 28. Messages in JClic Author

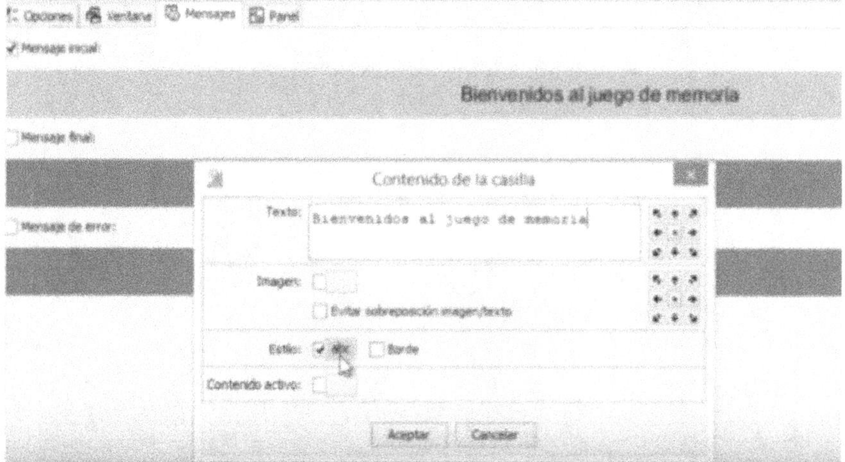

The panel tool allows to design the activity. To set an example, and as displayed in Figure 29, if teachers are interested in creating a memory game, they should specify the shape of the working panel (for example, rectangular), the number of rows (for example, 2), the number of columns (for example, 3) and the cell size (for example, 50width and 30 height).

Figure 29. Memory game JClic Author

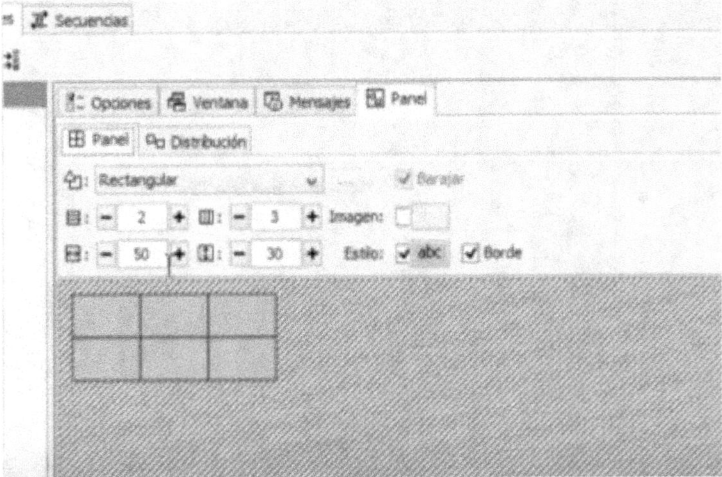

L2 English teachers can also design memory games that involve associating a word and its synonyms or opposites by simply typing in the target word or by associating an image with a word. If teachers decide to include one image per cell in Figure 29, they should be saved in the activity file where the activity was created (for instance, "countable nouns".

Figure 30. Adding images in JClic Author

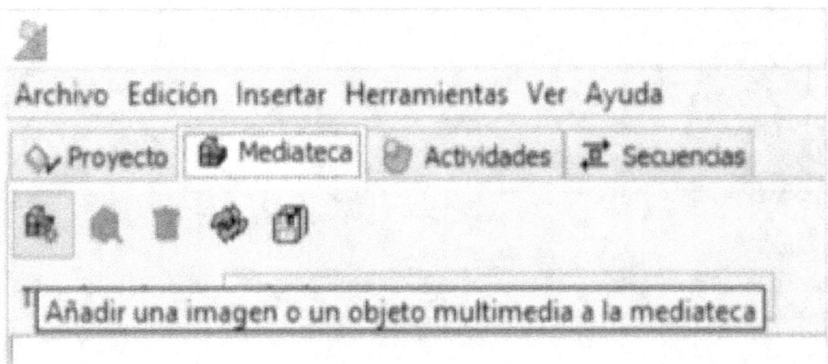

After saving the images, add them in the *Mediateca*, click on *Actividades* and insert an image per cell. As discussed earlier, if you are not going to work with text in the cells, it is unnecessary to include it in the text box.

Figure 31. Panel window in JClic Author

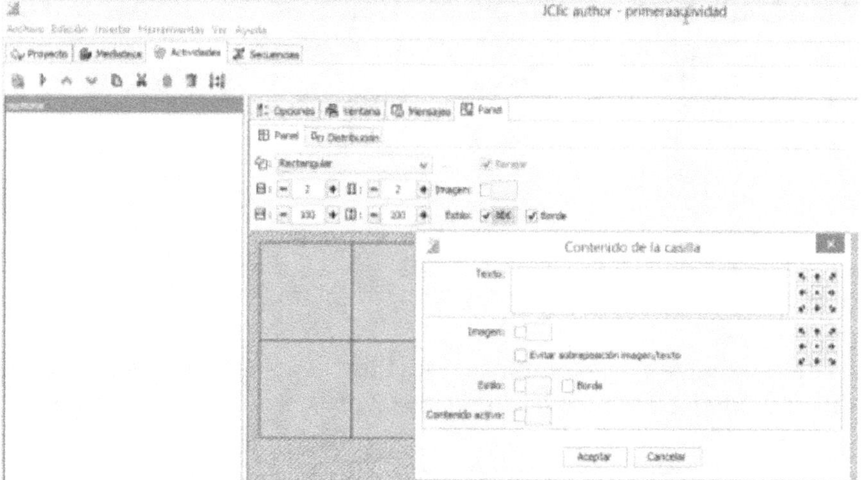

When clicking on the alternative content option (see *contenido alternativo* in Figure 31), it might seem that the images have disappeared. However, this is not the case since typing in the answers that correspond to each image is required. Therefore, click on each image cell and write the word. If you do not remember the order of the images, unclick the alternative content option. Once the task has been designed, click on play to check the game and save your activity as a web page (or .html format) which is the recommended option for teaching, or as a folder in the JClic library (see *Instalador del Proyecto*). As illustrated in Figure 32, go to the JClic program that was installed and open the activity that you have created; click on the library (see *bibliotecas*) > edit > main menu > search for the folder "uncountable nouns" > select the .zip uncountable nouns file. Finally, close all the windows and the activity will appear on the main JClic window with the icon you selected before.

Figure 32. JClic library

Other illustrative examples of further tasks that can be created via JClic include jigsaw puzzles and crosswords, as depicted in Figure 33.

Figure 33. Jigsaw puzzle and crossword designed by JClic

Ardora is an ICT teaching tool that allows the creation of different types of grammar-oriented lexical-oriented tasks, namely, crosswords, fill in the blanks, outlines and word searches. It also offers multimedia tools such as image zooming, mp3 or mp4 player and a gallery of images. Furthermore, it offers other collaborative resources for students, namely, annotations, chat, collective album, comments, file management, timeline and poster.

Ardora is available online at http://webardora.net/index_cas.htm. As shown in Figure 34, in order to create an activity, click on file (see *archivo*) and new activity (see *nueva* actividad). There is a wide range of activities available in Ardora, namely, graphic activities (for instance, album, graphic panels, puzzle or coloring according to a legend), word games, self-dictations, associations, classifications, ordering, selection, tests, outlines, among others.

Figure 34. Range of activities in Ardora

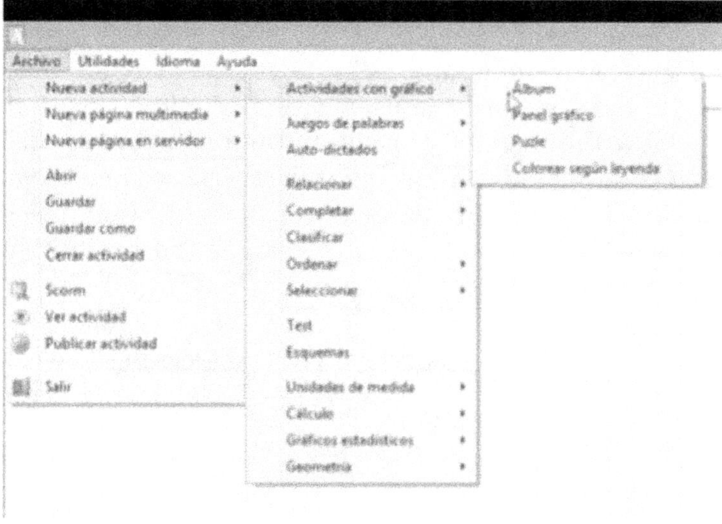


If we design an activity for L2 English learners to learn English vocabulary related to body parts. As depicted in Figure 35, we click on file (*archivo*) > graphic panel (*panel gráfico*) > choose the picture that has been previously saved in your computer. Then, double click on the body parts to type in the target vocabulary (for instance, arm, hair, mouth) and select how to guess the words by (a) selecting the word; (b) typing in the word; or (c) typing in the word with an arrow.

Figure 35. Body part identification in Ardora

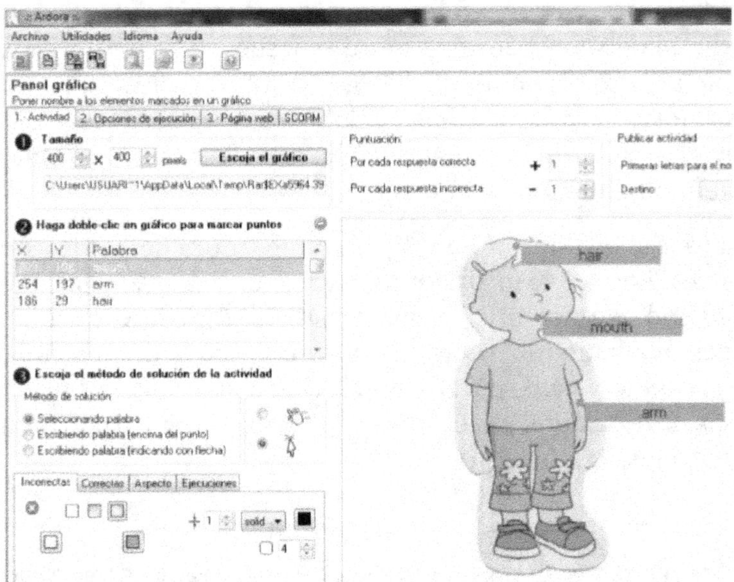

In the execution window, and as illustrated in Figure 36, you can limit the response time, reward the user with extra time (for example, 30 seconds), show the number of right and wrong answers, include the score and include messages for congratulating (for example, well-done), timing (for example, no more time) and chances (for example, there are no more tries). The three types of messages can be displayed with sound.

Figure 36. Execution options in Ardora

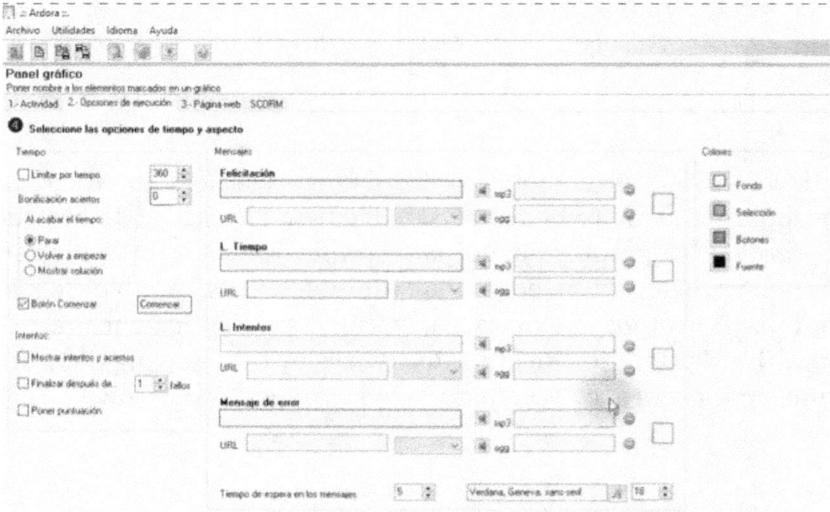

The webpage window depicted in Figure 37 is used to type in the header of the activity (for example, identify the body parts) and the title of the window (for instance, body parts).

Figure 37. Webpage window in Ardora

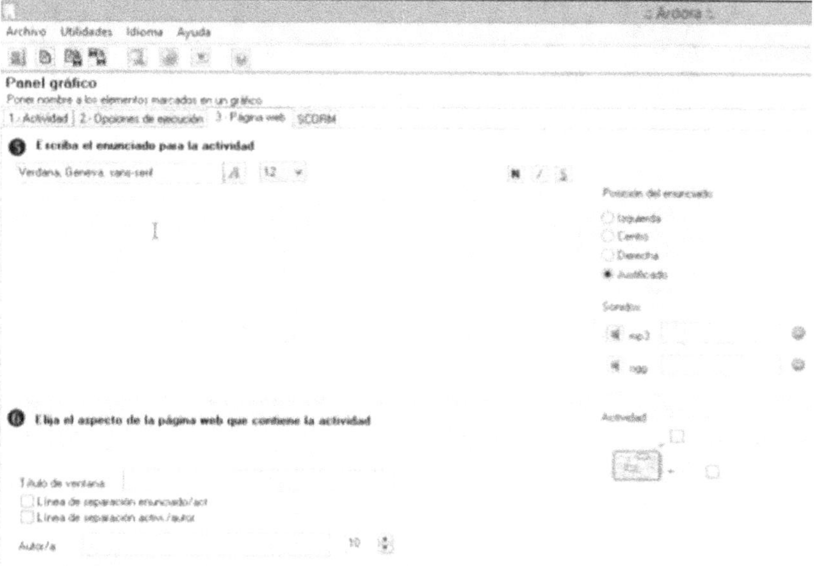

Finally, the SCORM window that appears in Figure 37 above allows to restart the activity once it is completed and keep the previous score if the activity has been restarted. Then, click on view the activity (that is, on the eye icon). You can save the activity as a file or as a html web (recommended for classrooms). The latter requires to indicate the folder where the activity is going to be saved (*actividad window > destino*) and then click on publish the activity (file (*archive*) > publish activity (*publicar actividad*)) so that the activity gets downloaded again.

Webquestions is a free software created by Daryl Rowland. It needs to be downloaded from ttp://www.aula21.net/webquestions/. Figure 38 shows the homepage of the program.

Figure 38. Webquestions homepage

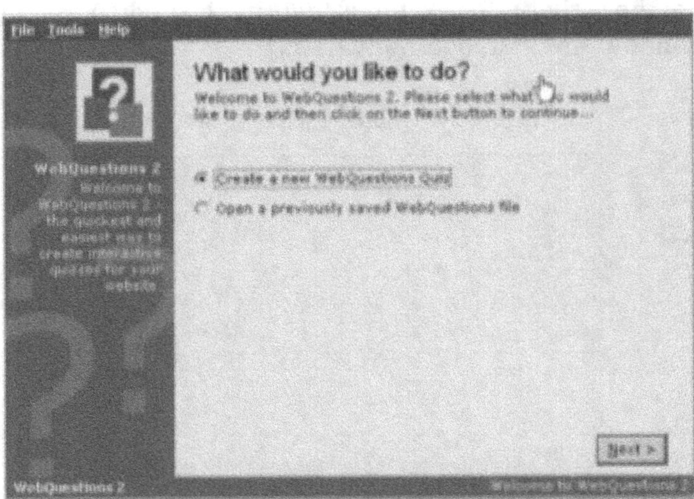

Ardora is an ICT tool that allows to create interactive questionnaires in html (or webpage) format. As depicted in Figure 39, four types of answers can be combined in one questionnaire, namely, free answer, hidden, word, multiple choice and true-false.

Figure 39. Types of questions in Ardora

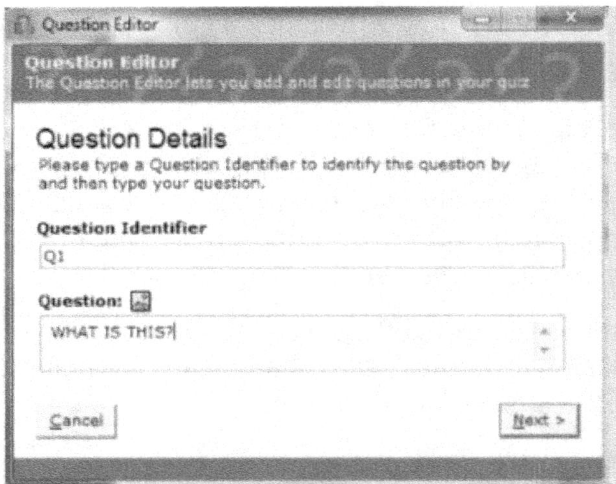

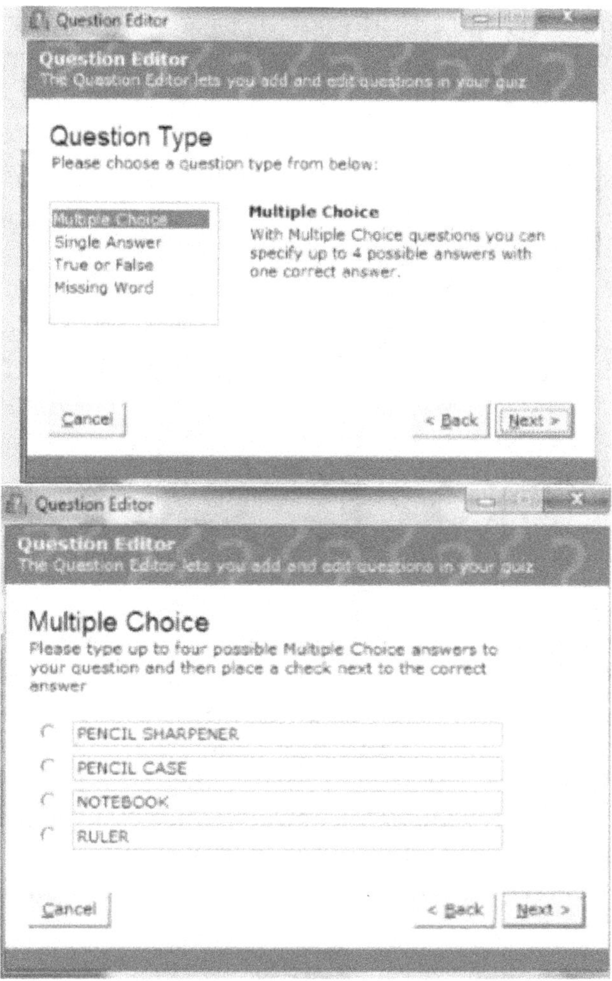

Hotpotatoes is a set of six authoring tools created by the Research and Development team at the University of Victoria (Canada). Teachers do not need to know about the so-called XHTML or JavaScript codes to use the program. Rather, they simply enter their data in texts, questions and answers and the program will create the webpages for them. Hotpotatoes requires to be downloaded from the following URL: https://hotpot.uvic.ca/index.php#downloads. Users are prompted to register when they start the application. This process simply asks you for your name and stores it in the system registry. Your name will be inserted into the exercises you create identifying you as the exercises' author. Furthermore, a username must be inserted to unlock all the features of the programs. The authoring tools will also handle Unicode so that you can create exercises in any language or in a mixture of languages.

As illustrated in Figure 40, Hotpotatoes consists of six authoring tools, namely, JCloze, JQuiz, JMatch, JCross, JMix and The Masher.

Figure 40. Hotpotatoes authoring tools

JQuiz is used for the design of gap-filling exercises and include multiple-choice and short answers. Specific feedback can be provided both for right and wrong answers or distractors. The learner can ask for a hint in the form of a free letter from the answer. As shown in Figure 41, the Cat Quiz exercise aims to answer how many lives a cat has. There are boxes for four potential answers to the question. By clicking on the top arrow next to the question allows to enter a new question. If more answers are added, the lower pair of up/down buttons are used to scroll through the correct answers. When all the data are complete, the data file is saved.

Figure 41. The Cat Quiz in JQuiz

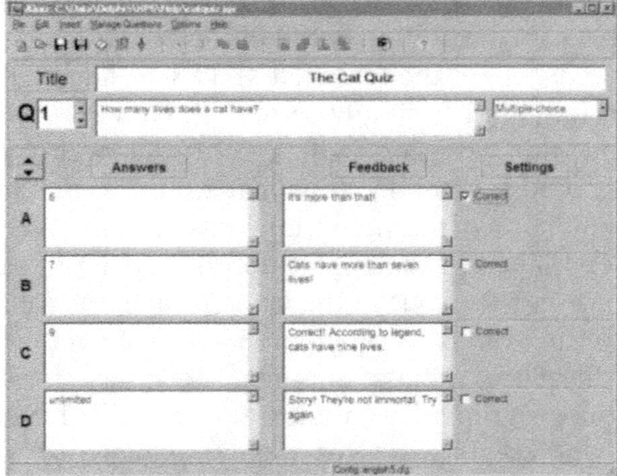

JCloze allows to create unlimited correct answers that can be specified for each gap. Learners can ask for a hint and automatic scoring is also included. As shown in Figure 42, when a word is gapped, it aims to hide the target word to be typed in. On the other page of the configuration dialogue box, use the drop-down list instead of the textbox in the output and, if you choose this option, each gap will show as a drop-down list instead of textboxes consisting of a list of all the gapped words in the exercise and, therefore, the hint button will not be shown. There is no need for hints if the words are all shown in the list.

Figure 42. Gap-fill exercise grid with JCloze

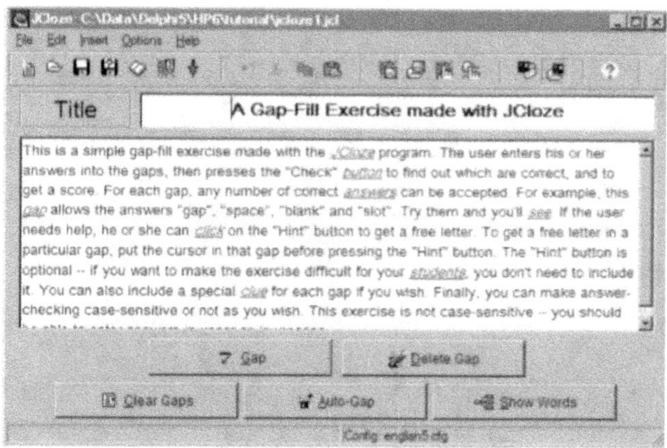

JCross is used to elaborate crossword exercises. A grid of any size is provided, and learners can ask for a hint. As illustrated in Figure 43, when you have created your grid, you can click on the add clues button to enter clues for all your words.

Figure 43. Crossword with JCross

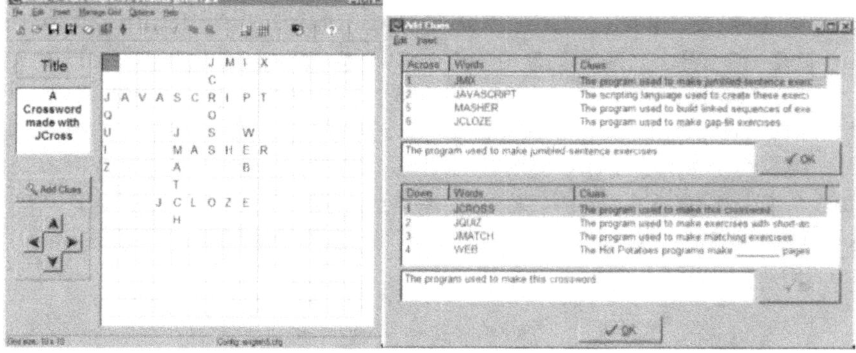

JMix aims to design mixed-up sentence exercises that include as many different correct answers as desired. A hint button allows students to request a free letter if help is needed. As depicted in Figure 44, sentences are broken down into separate segments, making them as big or as mall as you like. In order to carry this out, put each segment on a separate line. Note that the comma and the period are also on separate lines and they become separate segments. If quotation marks are required, double quotations ("") are used.

Figure 44. Jumble-sentence with JMix

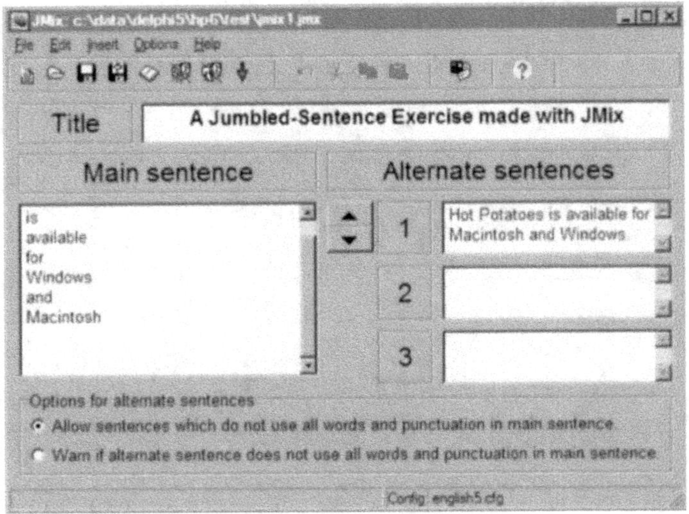


JMatch allows to create matching or ordering exercises. A list of fixed items (pictures or text) appears on the left and the jumbled items appear on the right. It can be used for matching vocabulary to pictures or translations, or for ordering sentences to form a sequence or a conversation. As shown in Figure 45, JMatch includes different output options: (a) the drag-and-drop output that allows to include pictures in both the left hand (fixed) items and the right-hand (draggable) items. It is recommended to use the drag-and-drop output if you have fewer than 12 items and preferably more than 8 since this option is difficult to do if the page is too big for the users' screen as they will have to scroll around quite a lot. Flashcards are an effective activity to help memorize the matching items. Feedback is limited to right and wrong answers and users are given a score.

Figure 45. Ordering exercise with JMatch

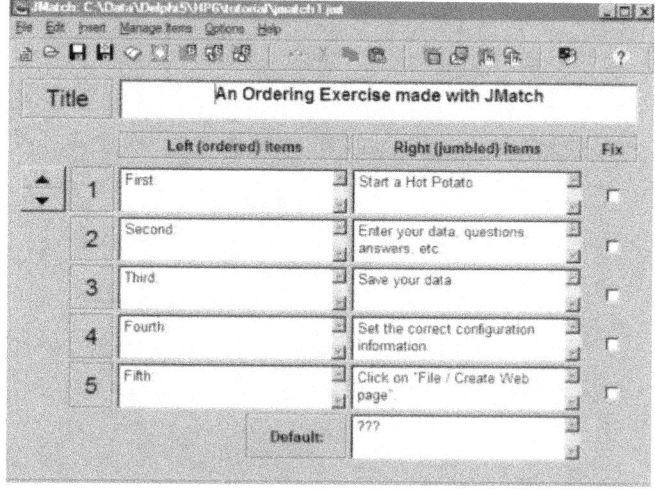

Each program saves files with its own extension, namely, .jqz (JQUIZ), .jcl (JCloze), .jcw (JCross), .jmx (JMix) and .jmt (JMatch).

The Masher is a tool designed to create complete units of material in one simple operation. Sequences of exercises are created in one go and the program sets the URLs automatically through Next Exercise navigation buttons.

Therefore, Hotpotatoes enables teachers to create web-based teaching tasks of several types:

a. Multiple-choice answers

b. Short answers

c. Jumble sentence (https://hotpot.uvic.ca/wintutor6/jmix1.htm)

d. Crosswords (https://hotpot.uvic.ca/wintutor6/jcross1.htm)

e. Matching or ordering (https://hotpot.uvic.ca/wintutor6/jmatch1.htm)

f. Gap-fill (https://hotpot.uvic.ca/wintutor6/jcloze1.htm)

g. Quiz (https://hotpot.uvic.ca/wintutor6/jquiz1.htm).

The exercises are standard web pages using XHTML code and JavaScript for interactivity.

Hotpotatoes also allows to include a reading text in a separate frame next to the quiz, as shown in Figure 46. Reading texts cannot be included if you have selected the drag-and-drop output from JMix and JMatch because the reading text may be typed in directly in the program or it can be imported from an external webpage.

 

Figure 46. Add a reading text

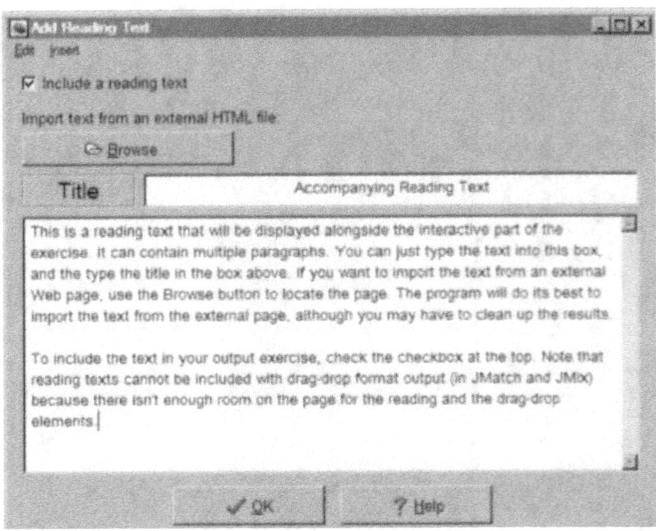

A timer can also be added from the timer tab of the configuration screen. Check the checkbox to include the timer and set the time limit in minutes and seconds. When the timer runs out, the student's work so far will be scored, and the score will be displayed.

It is also possible to insert images or links into the webpages, as depicted in Figure 47. Click on the insert menu > picture > picture local file. You will not see the image until you actually compile the page.

Figure 47. Adding a graph

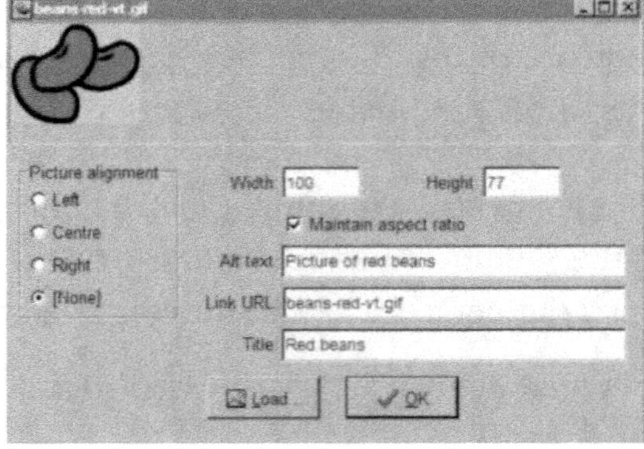

You may also wish to insert a link to another webpage in one of the fields in your exercise. As shown in Figure 48, click on the insert menu > link > link to web URL. You can use these link functions to add sound and video to your pages.

Figure 48. Insert a link

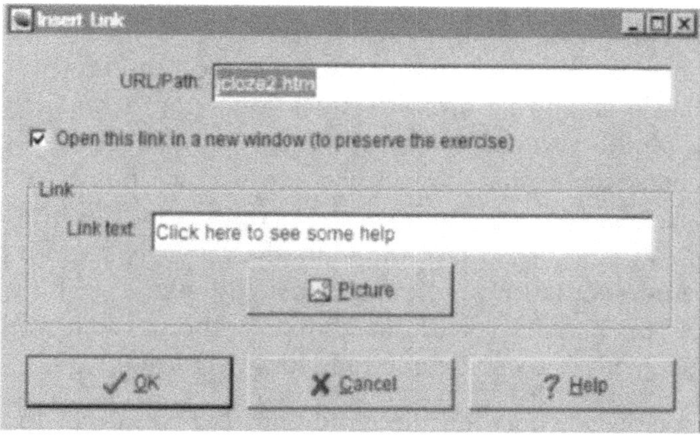


Hotpotatoes also allows to add sounds and videos. One of the options is by adding a link. Alternatively, sounds and videos can be uploaded from a local sound file. Click on the target question and then click on insert > link > link to local file. Then, press OK to bring up the open file dialog box. Find your sound file and select it, then press open. In the link text box, type an appropriate piece of text such as "click here to listen to the text" and press OK.

When your data are ready, and you have checked the configuration information, you are ready to create a webpage. Use the create webpage commands accessible through the file menu or the toolbar. You can post this file on your server and the exercise will appear when you load it. When you save the output, if you enter a file name containing a space, the program will not accept it.

How can we link a series of exercises? First of all, use the next exercise, contents and back buttons. In any of the six potatoes, click on configuration > buttons tb > set the three buttons above (you can decide if you want to include these buttons). You have to tell the program where the next exercise and the contents page actually are so that the button can jump to them. First, enter the URL (http:/...) to the next exercise in the correct box, then do the same with the contents page. For example, we are going to link a page called exercise1.htm to exercise2.thm as one folder. In order to do so, open the first page in your potato, go to the configuration screen (buttons tab) and make sure "include next exercise button" is checked. Then, enter exercise2.htm in the next exercise URL textbox, press OK and then compile your webpage. You should see a next exercise button on the page, click on it and the browser will go to exercise2.htm. Nevertheless, if all this is complicated to you, you have to look at the masher, which is designed to do this kind of linking automatically.

Hotpotatoes allows to complete exercises on the Internet or printed out. The tasks can be exported to educational platforms such as Dokeos, Helvia or Moodle. Nevertheless, one of the drawbacks of Hotpotatoes is that it needs to be installed in a computer so that activities can be created. Also, if we want to have the activities on the Internet so that students can complete them individually, they need to be hosted in a server. And, sometimes, students usually use the hint button to complete the activities without thinking about them and, thus, the pedagogical aim of these exercises is somewhat null.

Other resources host learning and teaching resources for L2 English learners such as Isabel Pérez (www.isabelperez.com) and Ego4u (www.ego4u.com).

## 2. ICT IN INTERPERSONAL COMMUNICATION

There are a lot of ICT tools that enhance interpersonal communication. One of them is eTwinning (www.etwinning.net) that enables communication among different people from different cultures. It was created by the European Commission. As can be consulted in the eTwinning platform homepage illustrated in Figure 49, schools can share information and knowledge, integrate the European citizenship and the linguistic or the cultural richness. Schools partners can only be added if they accept you as contacts. It has hot more than 12,000 European schools registered and more than 74,000 members.

Figure 49. ETwinning platform homepage

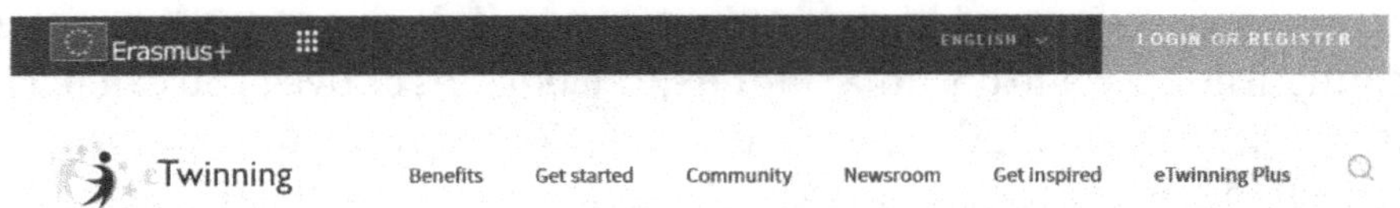


Collaborative work in multilingual school projects is fostered by eTwinning. For example, students of different nationalities can work on different projects within a big project. The classroom is the eTwinning space.

Epals also offers the possibility to establish contacts in several languages (for example, Spanish). We refer the reader to Figure 19 as the functionality of this platform has been previously discussed.

Videoconferences are a means of synchronic communication as they favor real-time interaction. Different types of resources can be added, namely, videos, interactive screens, the Internet and reading documents. Furthermore, videoconferences allow to record so that the content can be displayed at different times. Several applications in educational activities should be discussed (De Benito Crosetti and Salinas Ibáñez 2016):

a. Distance education training
b. Interaction (office hours, organization of activities, meetings) with students that are located in different geographical settings
c. Collaboration and communication in projects
d. Collaborative learning
e. Interaction with experts and teachers to share teaching and sharing experiences
f. Exposing learners to English native speakers and facilitating cultural exchanges

Some examples of videoconferences and their corresponding functioning tools are summarized in Table 2.

Table 2. Videoconferences

| Tool | Save conver-sation | Send a file | Share screen | Chat | Allowance of more than two users |
|---|---|---|---|---|---|
| **Ichat** (only Apple) (https://www.apple.com/la/ support/ichat/index.html) | X | X | X | X | X |
| **Ovoo** (https://oovoo.softonic.com/) | X | X | X | X | X |
| **Vsee** (only phone) (https://play.google.com/store /apps/details?id=com.vsee.vse e.release&hl=es) | X | X | | X | X |
| **Adobe Connect** (3 users for free; more users non-free) (https://www.adobe.com/ products/adobeconnect/ meetings.html?origref=https% 3A%2F%2Fwww.google.com %2F) | | X | X (and it also provide s a whiteb oard by default) | X | X |

| Tool | Save conver-sation | Send a file | Share screen | Chat | Allowance of more than two users |
|---|---|---|---|---|---|
| **Tokbox** (it offers 10$ in free credits-up to 10 users) (https://tokbox.com/account/user/signup) | X | X | | X | X |
| **Connecta 2000** (http://www.connecta2000.com/) | X | X | X | X | X |

Nevertheless, ICT tools involve some drawbacks such as (a) the cost of the tools (although it depends on the type of videoconference that we use in which case the cost is reduced); (b) lack of teachers' experience in the use and this requires more effort for preparation; (c) the need that the teacher and the student have developed a minimum competence to manage technical tools; (d) technical quality of the image and the sound (although the quality depends on the features of the tools that are used and it generally implies an image delay); and (e) teachers need a good didactic preparation to achieve students' participation and interaction.

## 3. ICT IN SEARCHING AND ANALYZING INFORMATION

There are several projects and ICT tools that allow to search and analyze information on the Internet about a specific topic. For example, we can formulate questions in forums, as it is the case of the ESL base forum available in https://www-eslbase.com/forum depicted in Figure 50. It hosts a wide range of different previously arranged subject teaching English areas such as training and courses, grammar, vocabulary and methodology. Log in is required to create a post in ESL base.

Figure 50. ESL base TEFL forum

As depicted in Figure 51, distribution lists are another example of specialized topic-related discussions. Such is the Case of LINGUIST list (https://linguistlist.org/LL/subs-index.cfm), an international Linguistics community online for those who are interested in information regarding language and language analysis in the field of Linguistics. This community is run by Linguistic students and faculty members.

Figure 51. The LINGUIST list subscription

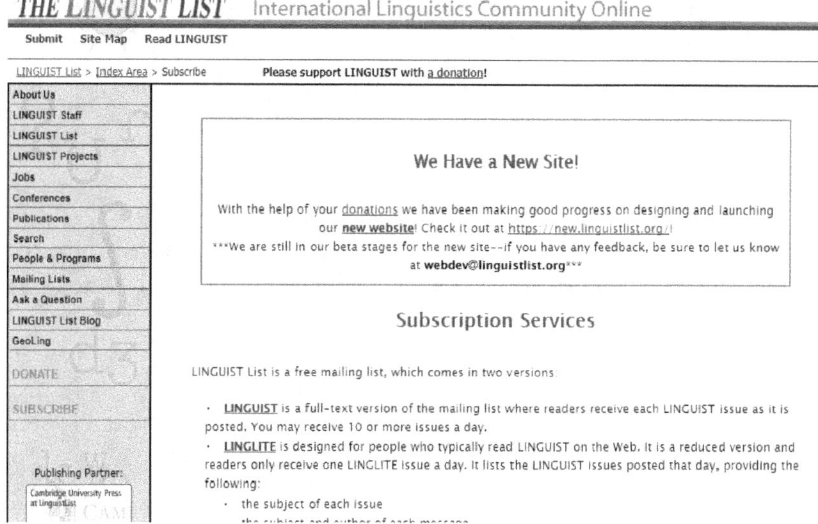

As for ICT platforms that enhance group design of knowledge, Flickr (www.flickr.com) enables the publication of your own pictures and explore other users' pictures via the search engine. You can search by topic, by people or by groups. It needs registration. Figure 52 shows a personalized Flickr platform.

Figure 52. Flickr platform

YouTube also allows group design of knowledge as we can comment on other users' videos, as depicted in Figure 53. In order to carry out this task, registration is not needed. However, if we are interested in subscribing to receive video updates from YouTube channels, registration is needed.

Figure 53. Users' comments on YouTube

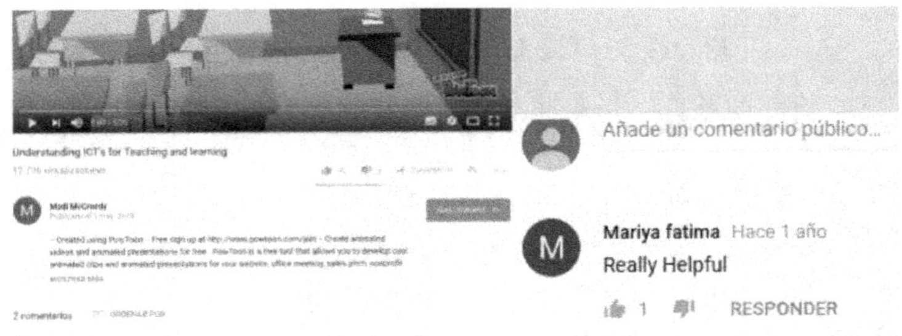

Wikipedia (www.wikipedia.org) boosts learners to contribute with new entries or edit old ones. Registration is needed to conduct these tasks.

Figure 54. Wikipedia

L2 English learners can also publish their work. Before completing this project, they should previously think about the purpose, the audience and how (for instance, a webpage, a blog, a wiki, a video or a podcast).

An example of a blog includes Ciberespiral (ciberespiral.net/edublogs). It aims to reflect on the use of ICT tools in education. Thus, it is addressed to teachers, researchers and students.

Digital story telling is another form of publishing school tasks (Fumero et al. 2007; Gargallo López and Suárez Rodríguez 2003). It refers to using new digital tools to help people to tell their own stories. With the emerging technologies, it is easier to benefit from this type of format given that we can reach a wider audience of readers. Digital story books can include music, pictures, videos to our narratives and are highly motivating for the so-called digital native generation. Indeed, they appeal to different types of learning styles. Furthermore, they develop communication and multimedia skills and engage learners in their own learning process and creativity abilities. Overall, digital story telling books can be easily published online.

One of the ICT tools that generates story telling books is Voicethread (https://voicethread.com). It is an effective tool for L2 English listening and speaking activities. Learners can leave comments or assess each other's work, write stories that go with the images they see, as illustrated in Figure 55. For example, L2 English teachers or students can give instructions regarding how to get to the train station or give advice while an image is being displayed.

Figure 55. Voicethread task

Zimmertwins (https://zimmertwinsatschool.com) is a site that allows to make your own videos and requires to sign up. L2 English teachers can provide students with dialogues so that they can design their own cartoons using this tool. Nevertheless, cartoons are also available in the platform and, thus, students can make use of them without having to create them from scratch, as seen in Figure 56. In particular, movies can be created on any topic by selecting and adding clips to the story. Cartoons should be picked in the scene, where they are and what prompts and dialogues they require. The students' movies will be displayed on the class-movies page

Figure 56. Zimmertwins and cartoons design

Webquests were created in 1995 by Bernie Dodge, a professor of the University of San Diego along with his colleague Tom March. They are a type of guided activity that is conducted by using the Internet resources that are previously selected by the teacher. Webquests are created so that learners can develop skills related to online information use successfully through analysis, creation, judgment or summary tasks while learning about a specialized field of study. They are framed in the so-called constructive approach given that the teacher is the facilitator and knowledge mediator when compared to the learner that builds his/her own knowledge by working in an autonomous manner. The webquests methodology is based on research and collaborative work, taking advantage of the resources that the Internet offers as a source of information (Adelle 2004; Rank et al. 2011).

In Webquests, although the Internet is the main source of information, learners are fostered to carry out tasks oriented to research and learn from insights. Learners will build their own learning from the investigation they conduct from the Internet resources that teacher provide. Thus, learners experience active learning and learn how to select useful information, be critical and develop creative skills in completing a task. In other words, they learn to learn.

Webquests consist of six main parts, namely, introduction, task, process, assessment, conclusion and resources. The introduction is a short text that presents the learning setting and involves the topic, the aim, the content and the resources. The introduction is usually formulated as a problem-solving task or a project to be designed.

The task presents the objectives and the approach adopted. It must determine whether the task should be done individually or in groups and what roles are allocated to each group member. Tasks should encourage students' reflection and the development of competences that go beyond the learning process of the task. Although the Internet resources are not repeated, learners are asked to reflect on them, draw conclusions, give their opinion and create something new. Examples of tasks include a multimedia presentation, a written report, a conceptual map, a flyer, an album or a graph. The target topic may include differences between two cultures, the analysis of the advantages and the disadvantages to carry out a project, elaborate a poster for the school, among others. Therefore, tasks could imply searching for information, reporting information, designing, creative production, persuasive activities, self-learning, analyzing, judging or scientific tasks.

The process describes how learners should complete the task. It includes Internet references (that is, websites) in each step to solve the final task. Strategies to divide tasks could be divided into subtasks and a description of each student's roles is required.

The assessment of the webquest should consider both the final result of the task as well as the process that has been followed to achieve it. Assessment matrices or rubrics should be used to evaluate effort and interest, level of topic understanding, learning strategies, skills to be developed, the use of ICT tools to construct knowledge, the quality of the final outcome, among others. The student will ultimately receive feedback from the teacher. An example of an assessment rubric is depicted in Table 3. Other examples of rubrics are available in platea.pntic.mec.es/erodri1/TALLER.htm#RUBRI.

Table 3. Assessment rubric

| SCORE | EXCELLENT | GOOD | OK | BAD |
|---|---|---|---|---|
| Search for information | All the information is selected and organized | Most of the information is selected and organized | Very little information is selected and organized | No information is selected and organized |
| Pictures, graphs and drawings | A lot of information is selected and organized | A few pictures and other graphs facilitate understanding of the topic | Some pictures and other graphs facilitate understanding of the topic | No pictures and other graphs are included |
| Clarity | Each section has an introduction, a main body and a conclusion | Nearly all sections have an introduction, a main body and a conclusion | Most sections have an introduction, a main body and a conclusion | Less than half of all sections have an introduction, a main body and a conclusion |

Rubistar is a rubrics generator for webquests, available in http://rubistar.4teacher.org. It formats the different assessment criteria in tables, enabling learners to know what factors they will be evaluated in. The rubric can be displayed in English or in Spanish. However, the Spanish translation is not complete since, in the middle of the process, it changes to English again. In order to create an assessment rubric, registration is need (fill in your personal data such as post code, password, email and click on create account). If we do not live in the US, we should type in the post code 99999.

The conclusion is a summary of the task and a reflection on the process and the results achieved. Suggestions regarding the expansion of the completed task should be discussed.

The resources are a list of websites (articles, newspapers, videos, among others) selected by the teacher to help learners in the task completion process. Resources can be divided so that some of them can be examined by the whole group while others can be allocated to each student's subgroups given that subgroups will adopt a specific role. Students can be provided with several websites that revolve around the same topic. This requires comparing, analyzing and summarizing data from different resources.

Why are webquests relevant in the classroom? One of the answers involve the development of strategies for searching for information based on the information available on the Internet. Also, they involve ideal typological tasks to integrate the digital competence, are built around a task that entails processing, searching, selecting, analyzing and summarizing information. The task should go beyond answering questions, cutting and pasting information that is already shared and published on the Internet. Furthermore, learners already have preselected online resources and can work in groups or individually along a wide range of sessions (from one week to several weeks).

Here is a list of webquest examples that target L2 English learning:

- **Aula21**: http://www.aula21.net/tercera/otrosidiomas.htm
- **Isabel Pérez**: http://www.isabelperez.com/rosaparty.htm
- **Portal WebQuest (en inglés):** http://webquest.org/
- **Dear Agony Aunt:** http://www.xtec.cat/eoiterrassa/ Departaments/MyAgonyAuntWebquest/index.htm
- **Symbols of England:** http://zunal.com/introduction.php? w=220290

Aula21 was created in November 2002 by the teachers Francisco Muñoz Peña and Alejandro Valero. It is a system that generates webquests online, as available in http://www.aula21.net/tercera/ listado.htm. The system generates a code in a single webpage in which the user has to use the sliding bars to access the sections of the webquest. Thus, that page is required to be later uploaded to the server that the user has available (namely, free, personal hosting or in the school/university) along with the corresponding images. The steps to design a webquest are detailed below:

1. Click on http://www.aula21.net/Wqfacil/webquest.ht, and fill in the fields: title of the project, author, level, email, description, keywords, introduction, task, process, resources, assessment, conclusion and credits

2. All these fields (except author, email and level) are optional. If you leave them in blank, they will not be displayed on the generated website.

3. Type in your data. Include a brief description of the created website and this helps search for this website in the web searchers. Also, type in a few keywords separated by commas; they will serve as search engines to classify our website and for users to visit it. You can change the font, the color of the text and the background. If you want to use a color that is not available, a HTML alphanumeric code is needed, as detailed in http://www.aula21.net/cazas/webcolours.htm. You can also change the background image to make it more appealing and increase the student's motivation. In order to specify an image for the background, type in the file name that will be included in the field *Textura* as imagename.gif (or the corresponding extension). Images can be included in all the section of our webquest (recall that all these image files are in the folder *Mi_WebQuest*.

4. To set an example of how to type in data in the introduction section, every time we create a new line or a full stop, we include the corresponding code at the end (namely, <br>). For bolded words, the code <b>*negrita*</b>, we should replace the word *negrita* by the text that you want it to appear as bold. For example, if we want "webquest" to appear in bold, we should type in <b>webquest</b>. In the case of italicized words, the code <i>*cursiva*<i> should be placed by the text that you want it to appear in italics.

5. When typing in the resources, Aula21 allows the inclusion of up to 15 URLS (websites).

6. Once the project is elaborated, you can change the pre-established printing options. Clik on "Create the website" (see *crear la webquest*) and you can see the result of your work on the same page. If you see that something needs to be modified, click on "back" (see *atrás*) once the modifications have been done. Then, click on "create the webquest" again. Do not worry if you do not see the attached images, you will see them when you open the final

file WebQuest.htm. You can print your page on file (see *archivo*) > print (see *imprimir*).

7. Save your website as a file or as a webpage in HTML format. In this way, the webpage can be shown in any browser and edited with any program (composer, dreamweaver, frontpage express). If you want to publish it on the Internet, upload the folder *MI_Webquest* on the server with all its content, files and images. The generated website meets the requirements of the world wide web consortium related to the HTML language 4.01. You can include this logo ( W3C HTML 4.01 ) at the end of the created page or validate the page on W3C: http://validator.w3.org/.

Aula21 is translated into six languages, namely, Spanish, Italian, English, Galician, Catalan and Basque and it is the first webquest free generator available online. It is a flexible program in that it allows to choose colors and letter size, as well as the insertion of images. Nevertheless, the user has to read and assimilate several instructions and he/she could make mistakes along the way. Also, there are no patterns available and, thus, the webquests generated will have an analogous pattern. Codes are created and it is not necessary to have a space for the website and upload the file generated on a hosting server.

Z Webquest is a free website that generates webquests. It also has a database that allows to host and search for webquests (for instance, to teach English). It is available in http://zunal.com/xbrowse.php?Curriculum=103&GradeLevel=101&Page=1. Apart from the five usual pages that webquests have, there are three extra pages, namely, a page for authors to introduce themselves, a page from reviews from other teachers and a page to include methodological orientations so that other teachers can consider them. The webquest can be printed in .pdf format and can include tutorials for the design of webquests.

## 4. WORKING WITH VIDEOS

Videos are highly motivating for L2 English learners and, specially, for those ones that are born as digital native citizens. Using videos to teach and to learn English may require the use of subtitles in the target language of the projection. How can we do that? We can use videos that already have subtitles, add subtitles to any video or include tests to videos.

If we use YouTube videos, we should type in the topic on the search dialogue (for instance, trumpet), click on the search options and, among the several options, choose "closed subtitles". Once you click on the search option, a list of videos will be displayed about the searching topic with integrated subtitles. Teachers can choose according to the students' interests, the topic, the length of the video, among other options. Below the image of the video, there is a small image highlighted with a square that is shown when the video is dubbed. This image allows to access a menu of subtitle languages in case there is more than one. With the command "subtitle actions", we can also (a) transcribe the audio (the program, based on voice recognition techniques, transcribes the oral messages of the video) and (b) translate the subtitles (YouTube shows the subtitles in the selected language; however, this tool has a less pedagogical effectiveness, that is, students run the risk of focusing on the translation rather than the spoken message). Nevertheless, the system in (a) and (b) is not highly accurate and needs improvement.

Other commands on YouTube involve trimming out some parts of the video, apply slow motion and blur faces to protect privacy (see https://support.google.com/youtube/answer/1388383?visit_id=1-636650016741102045350127049&7hl=en&rd=1) as well as including subtitles (see https://support.google.com/youtube/answer/2734796 ?hl=en&visit_id=1-6366500167411020453501270497&rd=1).

In order to add subtitles to your videos, you can use DotSub (http://dotsub.com) where registration is needed first. The translating process involves uploading the video from our computer > transcribe it > translate it > share it. Given that the most elaborated process is to find a video, go to http://keepvid.com, copy the URL from a YouTube video, paste it on keepvid and download it by following the instructions given. Then, go to DotSub > post a new video > complete the form and click on submit. In case of doubts, click on "watch a tutorial on uploading videos".

If we are interested in including tests to videos, it is important to link an exercise after the video is watched. In order to do so, use ESLVideo (www.eslvideo.com). Thus, we can use the tests (based on audios) that have been previously created by other teachers, then go to "looking for a quiz?" and type in any relevant word or phrase to search for (for example, greenhouse). Tests are grouped into proficiency level. Nevertheless, if we want to create our own video-test, we should register first, create a teacher code on the menu my account > classes > create/edit your teacher code > join class account. Students will type in the name of the class group they belong to on ClassID so that students can send teachers the test results. The steps to be followed are summarized below:

- Setp 1. In step 1, you will need the video embed code and URL. Copy the video embed code from YouTube and paste it in the quiz builder. Copy the YouTube URL and paste it in the Thumbnail Image Fetch Tool. Save the fetched image to your computer. Click the "browse" button and upload the thumbnail image.

- Step 2. Enter the quiz questions and answers, transcript and notes.

- Step 3. Note the quiz number. Students can quickly navigate to your quiz by using the "jump to a quiz" tool on the homepage. Your quiz has been added to your Teacher Page and to the archive (if it has more than five questions). You can edit your quiz at anytime from you account > quizzes page.

- Step 4. Embed the URL in a blog or in a virtual learning platform.

- Step 5. Check the menu "students grouped by class id" to see whether a student has signed in a class using our Teacher Code on the menu "Classes". From this moment, students can do our tests and send their scores. Scores appear on our account by clicking on the link "student scores".

## 5. OTHER MULTIMEDIA RESOURCES

Infographics are another effective ICT tool in the L2 English teaching classroom. They are graphic visual representations of information, data or knowledge aiming at presenting complex information in a quick and clear way. They make information easier to understand.

Infographics foster literacy skills since you go return to the source text(s) used n their design. They can be used to elaborate short pieces of information into something detailed. For instance, students can be given an infographic and asked to write an article starting from the information they have. In this way, they can practice their writing skills and are very useful for visual learners. Furthermore, learners access contextualized information in an appealing way, expand the lexical repertoire with an actual information source, have the support the support of a conversation starter (useful for conversational lessons as discussion points).

Infographics can replace hand-outs, help teach the English grammatical rules, provide a motivating way to set homework. For instance, learners can see the grammatical explanations and then play a related language game to test their understanding of the grammar. They also synthesize content knowledge and organize ideas, that is to say, learners analyze the most relevant information to be included. Indeed, infographics shift from passive consumers to content creators, encourage creativity and divergent thinking, develop learners' engagement with content, cultivate critical thinking and promote the authentic use of languages. They are shareable as .pdf, .png, .jpeg, tweeter, snap, among others.

Here is a list of examples of infographics used for L2 English learning:

a. Spelling mistakes: https://www.quora.com/What-are-some-great-free-infographics-for-teaching-English-as-a-secondlanguage

b. Monolingualism vs. Bilingualism: http://larryferlazzo.edublogs.org/2013/09/04/the-best-infographics-about-teachinglearning-english-as-a-second-or-third-language/

c. How to teach English: https://www.kaplaninternational.com/blog/how-to-teach-english-kaplan-infographic

d. Tips for a job interview: http://www.dailyinfographic.com/wp-content/uploads/2012/04/Anatomy-of-a-JobInterview.jpg

e. American vs. British English food related vocabulary: http://themetapicture.com/you-sound-like-youre-fromlondon/

f. Phrasal verbs: https://www.pinterest.es/pin/561683384753057941/

g. Idioms: http://www.grammar.net/wp-content/uploads/2012/02/12-love-idioms_small_ver3-01.png

h. Others: http://www.best-infographics.com/

The ICT tools that allow to create infographics from templates are detailed below:

a. Piktochart (https://piktochart.com/). It gives users a wealth of icons that help students communicate their ideas such as two circles (countable vs. uncountable nouns). You can add texts to the icons to provide meaning. Furthermore, it allows to upload images from the Internet such as a map.

b. Intogr.am (https://infogram.com/)

c. Canva (https://www.canva.com/es_es/)

d. Genial.ly (https://www.genial.ly/)

e. Visme (https://www.visme.co/)

f. Adioma (https://adioma.com/)

g. Google Draw (https://quickdraw.withgoogle.com/)

h. Smore (https://www.smore.com/)

i. Venngage (https://es.venngage.com/)
j. Easel.ly (https://www.easel.ly/)

The use of ICT tools in students with special educational needs should encourage their social, their educational and their cultural integration. In order for a student with special educational needs to use ICT resources correctly, it is essential to adapt the ICT tools (both hardware and software) to be used (Porràs and Salazar 2002; Toledo 2013). Therefore, students with special needs will require the following ICT tools:

a. Special keyboards
   (https://www.youtube.com/watch?v=Wdva_C-RGUk)
b. Braille printers
   (https://www.youtube.com/watch?v=vRubkWKWq68)
c. Special switches (https://www.youtube.com/watch?v=8SFKkx-NIDQ)
d. Zoom of font in screens for visual aid issues
e. Head pointer
   (https://www.youtube.com/watch?v=Co4EcSM50B0)
f. Joystick computer mouse
   (https://www.youtube.com/watch?v=3DR9fAQuOK8)
g. Eyed controlled mouse
   (https://www.youtube.com/watch?v=yCZ0BD3XiD4)
h. Touched screen computers
   (https://www.youtube.com/watch?v=IS0HPhNVssg)

While blind students can consult documents on the Internet by means of synthesizers and braille keyboards, students with visual issues can read the information by adjusting the color, the background contrast and the font or the letter size.

The teachers' role in selecting ICT tools in students with special needs should consider (a) students' profile (educational needs, capacities and skills, ICT knowledge); (b) ICT selection-curricular aspects (what are the aims? How is ICT going to be used? When? How is it going to be assessed?); and (c) the use of the appropriate ICT tool (standard or specific, hardware or software).

# Chapter 3

# The Internet and educational resources

## 1. THE INTERNET: A BRIEF BACKGROUND

The Internet is characterized by a network of computers (Reyzábal Manso and Santiuste Bermejo 2006). Its origins date back in the 1960s with the creation of a red called ARPANET in 1961. More specifically, ARPANET aimed to (a) transfer data; (b) send private and official emails related to the project (this is the onset of the email); (c) share IT resources; and (d) develop distribution lists. As will be discussed further in section 3, distribution lists are based on the email and the messages sent and received to/by a group of professionals that share similar interests. Distribution lists allow to distribute and exchange information to subscribes so as to encourage debate of ideas and experience.

ARPANET Is the predecessor of the Internet. In 1961, Leonard Kleinrock wrote about ARPANET in his doctoral dissertation entitled "Information Flow in Large Communication NETs". Kleinrock, along with other innovators such as Licklider, provided the backbone for the stream of emails and social media such as Facebook postings and tweets that are now shared only every day.

In 1969, the American Defense Department's Advanced Research Projects Agency Network (ARPANET) was founded. The funded researchers in ARPA developed many of the protocols used for the Internet communication that we have nowadays.

Historically, the use of the Internet evolved as follows (Anderson and Van Weert 2002; Rodriguez Terceño 2012; Sardelich 2006):

- **In 1965**: Two computers at the Massachusetts Institute of Technology Lincoln Lab communicate with one another
- **In 1972:** Beranek and Newman introduce the network mail
- **In 1973:** The term Internet is born

- **In 1974:** The first Service Provider (ISP) is born with the introduction of a commercial version of ARPANET, known as TELENET
- **In 1982:** The Internet Protocol (IP) emerges as the protocol for ARPANET
- **In 1983:** The Domain Name System (DNS) establishes the naming websites: .edu, .gov, .com
- **In 1990:** Tim Berners-Lee, a scientist at CERN develops the Hyper Text Markup Language (HTML)
- **In 1994:** Yahoo is created by Jerry Yang and David Filo, two electrical graduated engineers at Standford University
- **In 1995:** Amazon and eBay go live
- **In 1998:** The Google search engine is born
- **In 2003:** The blog publishing platform WordPress is launched
- **In 2004:** Facebook goes online, and Mozilla Firefox browser emerges
- **In 2005:** YouTube is launched
- **In 2006:** Twitter is launched by Jack Dorsey
- **In 2010:** The social media sites Pinterest and Instagram are launched

The onset of world wide web (www) was developed by the European Organization in Nuclear Research (CERN) in Switzerland. Two main browsers allowed the functioning of the www, namely, the NSCA Mosaic (the first one), Explorer by Microsoft and Communicator by Netscape. A wide range of multimedia tools were allowed to be used, namely, images, sound and video along with hyperlinks.

While the HTML or Hypertext Markup Language refers to the language (or the set of markup tags) used for describing webpages that are displayed in a browser, as shown in Figure 57, the HTTP or Hypertext Transfer Protocol allows to transfer information to the www, as seen in Figure 58.

Figure 57. HTML

```
function rx(){var ww=window.innerWidth;if(!ww){ww=
document.documentElement.clientWidth;};
dx=(ww-parseInt(xr.style.width))/2;i=-parseInt(xr.style.width)/2;if(dx<0
){i=-dx;dx=0;};xr.style.marginLeft=i+"px";};
window.onresize=rx;
</script>
<link rel="stylesheet" type="text/css" href=
"1htmlxaraweb.htm_files/default.css" /></head>
<body style="" onload="rx()">
<div id="xr" style="width: 1587px; height: 1123px; position:absolute;
top:0px; left:50%; margin-left: -794px; clip: rect(0px 1587px 1123px
0px);"><script type="text/javascript">var xr=document.getElementById(
"xr")</script>
<a href="Close | close" ><img src="1htmlxaraweb.htm_files/0.png" border=
"0" alt="" style="left: 579px; top: 370px; width: 85px; height: 27px;
position: absolute;"/></a><div style="left: 30px; width: 734.7px;
height: 120.0px;  position: absolute; font-size: 12pt; font-family:
Arial; text-align: left; top: 32px;"><div style="white-space: pre;"
><span style="left: 0px; top: -16px; position: absolute; white-space:
pre;">This is an example of the work that can be done in Xara with <span
 style=""><a href="http://thephotofinishes.com"  target="_blank" >HTML
</a></span> files. Lets fill with some Latin droll - </span><span
style="left: 0px; top: 2px; position: absolute; white-space: pre;">
venic vidi vici Caesar deducat prae vem importtantum; qui credit este
```

Figure 58. HTTP

A browser is a software application that guarantees information access on the www. When users access a webpage, the browser retrieves the information from a web server and displays it on the user's computer. Example of browsers include Google Chrome, Internet Explorer and Mozilla Firefox. All these browsers have a Uniform Resource Locator (URL). You can add your favorite webpages as bookmarks to speed up the access. As shown in Figure 59, the URL consists of four part, namely, the http protocol, the www subdomain, the webpage domain and the domain name system (DNS) such as .com, .es, .edu, among others.

Figure 59. URL

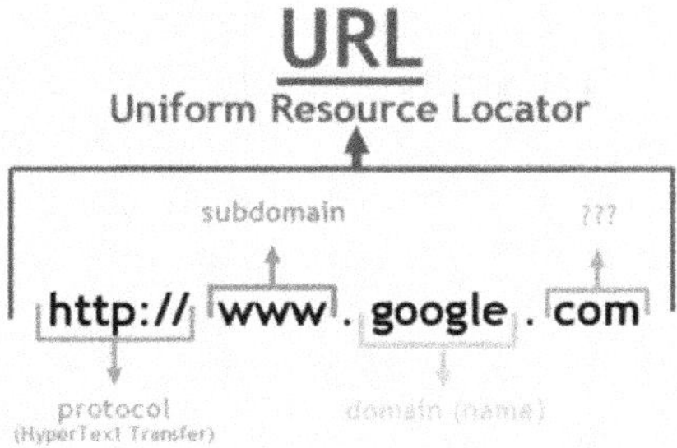

The Internet allows to access reading online newspapers such as The New York Times (www.nytimes.com) and The Guardian (www.theguardian.com) in English, or El País (www.elpais.es) and El Mundo (www.elmundo.es) in Spanish.

Furthermore, users can carry out online shopping in Amazon (www.amazon.es in Spain, www.amazon.co.uk in the UK and www.amazon.de in Germany), Bookfinder for second-hand books (www.bookfinder.com), among a varied and long list of sources.

When accessing search (drive) engines, users should make use of the so-called Boolean codes, namely, inverted commas when searching for the literal words, AND when combining two searches, OR when searching alternates (that is, one or the other) and NOT when discarding searches. Examples of search engines include Altavista, Ask, Google, Lycos, Ole, Pregunta and Terra, among others.

Most users do not have the knowledge of the resources available on the Internet and, more specifically, the licenses that lie behind the Internet in the use of online resources. For example, can I use this picture in my work? If I make a document public on the Internet, does it mean that users can distribute it and share it freely? The answer to these questions is determined by the <<licenses of use>> that determine how we can use the material that is available on the Internet and how to protect our own work and creations. It is crucial to know and respect the <<licenses of use>> to prevent inaccurate uses or break the law when making use of the resources. Thus, we should select the correct license for our own resources. By default, the law establishes that every piece of artistic, literary or scientific work is licensed by copyright. Nevertheless, if every resource is protected by copyright, this would mean that we could not reuse any type of content freely or without allowance. There are other open licenses that allow to copy, modify and redistribute the resources and they include copyleft, Creative Commons, free software or public dominion.

Copyright (©) involves a group of laws that are granted to authors' own works. It protects any original artistic, literary or scientific work that is considered as having intellectual nature. Authors have the right to copy, distribute, reproduce, exhibit and modify their work, that is, all the rights are reserved. The use of any author's creation without the author's permission can imply breaking the intellectual property rights. If that is the case, the author can take legal actions and, in the case of more serious cases, it is punished with prison or with a fine. Furthermore, authors have moral and property rights in relation to the use of their work. As for moral rights, authors' work is recognized, the integrity of the work is respected and, therefore, the work cannot be modified. Moral rights cannot be granted, sold or transferred. As for property rights, they involve any rights that deal with the exploitation of the work and belong to the author along his/her life and their heirs after the author's death during a short period of time (in Spain, 70 years). After this time span, the work belongs to public dominion.

Therefore, copyright protects scientific inventions (such as IT programs, databases or websites), literary or artistic productions (such as choreographies drama works, films, musicals, novels, paintings, pictures, poems or sculptures), logos and brands as well as drawings and industrial models (such as graphs, maps, patterns, plans or projects).

There are alternative licenses to copyright known as open licenses. They allow authors to grant some rights about their works and indicate that they can be used, modified and shared freely as long as the copyright is respected. Examples of open licenses include public dominion, copyleft and Creative Commons.

A piece of work has public dominion (☺) when the property rights expire. This occurs when the author (a) rejects the copyright of his/her work or (b) dies and the copyright period expires after his/her death. The piece of work can be used and modified freely as long as the author's moral rights are respected. If the piece of work is modified, a new copyright license can be established in which the new author acquires the property rights on it. However, the original author should be mentioned in the new modified work.

Copyleft (☺) eliminates the restrictions of distribution or modification imposed by the copyright. The only condition implies that the derived work has to keep the same author's rights when compared to the original work.

Creative Commons (☺) is a non-governmental organization whose aim is to help reduce the legal barriers of creativity through a new law and new technologies. It allows authors to grant some rights about their work and decide on the rights they want to grant. That is, authors can indicate the type of use that they want to allow for their own work freely and legally. As illustrated in Table 4, there are four basic rights in the Creative Commons license.

Table 4. Creative Commons' basic rights

| Icon | Right | Description |
|---|---|---|
|  | Attribution (BY) | Authorship acknowledgement in the use of the work |
|  | Share-alike (SA) | The creation of derived works is allowed as long as the same license is maintained |
|  | Non-commercial (NC) | The exploitation of the work is limited to NC use. This condition only affects those that use the work rather than the author |
|  | No derivative works (ND) | The modification of the work is not allowed to create a derived work |
|  | Attribution (BY) + commercial and non-commercial | Any exploitation of the work is allowed (copy, adapt or modify, redistribute), including the commercial use |
|  | Attribution-(BY) + non-commercial | The commercial use of the original copy or of the derived works are not allowed |
|  | Attribution-Share-alike (BY-SA) + commercial and non-commercial | The commercial use of the work and the possible derived ones is allowed. The latter should maintain the same type of license |
|  | Attribution-no derivative works (BY-ND) + commercial and non-commercial | The commercial use of the work is allowed but derived works are not allowed |
|  | Attribution-Non-Commercial-Share-alike (BY-NC-SA) + non-commercial | The commercial use of the original work or the derived works is not allowed. The latter should maintain the same type of license |
|  | Attribution-Non-Commercial-Non-derivative works (BY-NC-ND)-non-commercial | The commercial use of the original copy and f the derived work is not allowed |

Once the author decides on the type of license, the way of referring to it is as follows: Creative Commons license BY-NC-ND. Author: Name. We should also include the link to the Creative Commons website (www.creativecommons.org) so that users can be informed about the license conditions and the correct use of the resource.

Examples of reusable content with open licenses are displayed in Table 5.

Table 5. Type of license per ICT tool

| Online ICT tool | License | Description |
|---|---|---|
| Flickr (www.flickr.com/search/?q=&l=cc) | Creative Commons | Images → on the advanced search, select the option <<search content with CC license>> |
| Google (www.google.es) | Creative Commons | Images or other types of content → On the advanced search, select << rights of use>> and the <<use and share freely>> |
| Wikimedia Commons | Creative Commons | Pictures, diagrams, cartoons, music, audio, video, multimedia files |
| CC Search (http://search.creativecommons.org/) | Creative Commons | The original CC website offers searches for images, videos, websites and multimedia files |
| Mofguefile (http://mofguefile.com) | Creative Commons | A repository of free images (it is not necessary to cite the author) |
| Jamendo (http://jamendo.com) | Creative Commons | Music |

While teachers' resources can be applied copyleft and public dominion, the creation of software cannot be applied Creative Common licenses as it is the case of IT applications such as virtual labs or simulators, among others.

## 2. THE ELECTRONIC EMAIL

It offers quick transfer of information when compared to the conventional mail. In addition, it is a reliable and comfortable source of communication by means of a free account registration. Users can attach files.

Users can forward emails to several accounts. In the "to" field, we include the people that the message directly affects to and that you require action form. This field lets others know who is involved in the conversation and can be used for as may email addresses as desired.

The Carbon Copy (CC) field is used address the message users; however, the message is not directly involved to them. CC is used for users that do not need to act or reply to the message, but they are required to be informed.

The Blind Carbon Copy (BCC) field is used when you want other users to receive the message. However, you do not want the other recipients to know they received it. BCC is useful when sending an email to hundreds of users and you do not want them to see each other's email addresses.

Therefore, while the To and the CC lines allow the receivers' addresses, the BCC line, the receivers' addresses are not seen.

Examples of URLs that allow users to forward emails include Hotmail (www.hotmail.com), Outlook by Microsoft (www.outlook.com), Terra (www.terra.es), Yahoo (www.yahoo.es), among others.

The email can be applied to L2 English learning as a tool to exchange among students from many different countries.

## 3. DISTRIBUTION LISTS

Distribution lists require users to subscribe. Each subscriber will send a message that is distributed automatically among the rest of the subscribers.

They involve specific topics. Thus, when someone is interested in one of the topics, he/she should subscribe to that list and will receive information related to the specific target field. By sending an email to the list (recall that there is one single email), all the community members will receive it in their own email accounts.

Examples of distribution lists include (a) Rediris on www.rediris.es/list/, funded by the Spanish Ministry of Economy and

(b) LINGUIST list on http://linguistlist.org, specialized in languages (not just English) and general Linguistics, it hosts information about new articles and new books released, teaching practices, debates and doubts.

## 4. SCIENTIFIC INFORMATION RETRIEVAL

Academic information can be retrieved from university libraries such as the Spanish National library (www.bne.es), e-prints Autonomous University of Madrid (www.ucm.es/eprints/), Dspac@Cambridge at the University of Cambridge (https://www.repository.cam.ac.uk) and UNIA at the International University of Andalusia (http://dspace.unia.es/) for accessing thesis, research projects and academic articles.. Likewise, biographies and documents can be accessed in Instituto Cervantes (www.cervantes.es), Antonio Machado (www.abelmartin.com) and Juan Ramón Jiménez (www.fundacion-jj.es).

Other scientific information retrieval resources include the Centre of the Bergen University (www.hit.uib.no), literary works from the Gutenberg Project (www.promo.net/pg/) and Classical English authors. The latter entails resources related to Middle English Compendium (www.hti.umich.ed/mec) to access Middle English electronic dictionaries, texts via annual subscription or one free month access, as wee as Shakespeare's complete works (http://techtwo.mit.edu/ Shakespeare/ works.html).

## 5. ONLINE TEACHING RESOURCES

Before selecting L2 English teaching and learning resources available on the Internet, we should consider the aim, the content and the Internet access (Pereira Domínguez 2005; Salazar Noguera and Juan Garau 2009). The types of tasks selected need to be integrated in a coherent project, namely, music, booking flights and accommodation, organizing a trip, religion, the environment, checking the weather forecast, immigration, social exclusion and unemployment. In other words, the tasks structure may include listing in brainstorming and fact-finding, ordering and sorting, creative tasks, sharing personal experiences, problem-solving and comparing.

Lingolex (http://www.lingolex.com/espan.htm) generates flashcards for L2 English vocabulary learning. It also offers grammar explanations, speaking exercises, topic-related vocabulary lists. Furthermore, Lingolex hosts exchange programs and live conversations with English speakers as well as a list of language schools in the UK and Ireland for

L2 English teachers to take them into account for potential language exchange programs.

The Spanish Ministry of Education, Culture and Sport (https://intef.es/recursos-educativos/) includes books, exercises, a repository or images videos and audios as well as a platform to share teaching experiences. In turn, it provides a program to create teaching resources named ExeLearning.

The British Council (https://www.teachingenglish.org.uk/) provides songs, tests, listening exercises, reading comprehension tasks, lesson plans and webinars for L2 English learning. These resources are organized in terms of school levels, namely, Key Stage 1, Key Stage 2, Key Stage 3 and GSCE.

PDF drive offers English grammar books and many other L2 English resources. It is freely available in https://pdfdrive.net/english-grammar-books.html.

The BBC (www.bbc.co.uk/worldservice/learningenglish) provides a varied range of resources of L2 English learning and teaching. These resources entail grammar exercises (for example, the grammar gameshow in video format), grammar contrasts (for instance, English in a minute), short stories (for example, the experiment), news review, academic writing (for example, go to the distance task), every day speaking topics (for instance, English my way) and Shakespeare's works.

The USC library provides links to books, journals and other resources, as available in https://uscprimo.hosted.exlibrisgroup.com/primoexplore/search?query=any,contains,ict%20english%20teaching&tab=everything&search_scope=EVERYTHING&vid=01USC&lang=en_US&offset=0.

ClassTools (www.classtools.net) creates imaginary Facebook posts for study purposes, free games, interactive quizzes, crosswords, breaking news headlines, diagrams (see the Venn template) and timelines. It also provides a plagiarism checker. In the case of imaginary Facebook posts for study purposes, L2 English learners can design book plots, develop characters such as Joh Lennon in Figure XX, historical events, get started by entering the name at the top of the page, add friends, posts, comments and profile information. The Facebook post can be saved and edited later.

Figure 60. ClassTools' John Lennon Facebook post

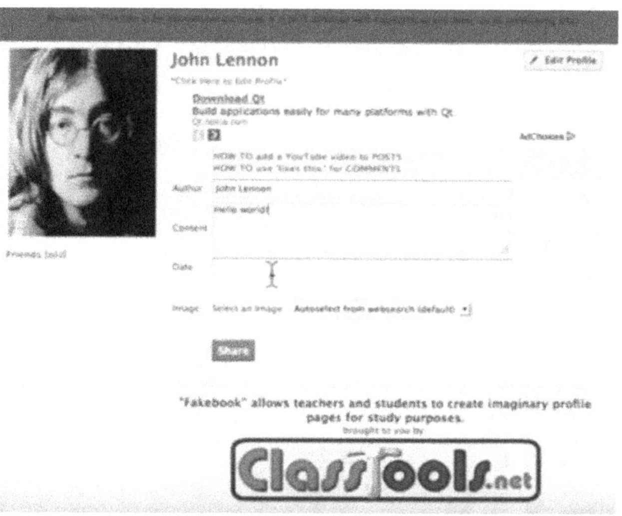

ClassTools also creates arcade games such as question/answer format that includes a minimum of 10 questions or associations of concepts that we would like students to learn. Thus, arcade games display a question-answer written format such as what is Wagner's name?*Richard. The asterisk is required before the answer. Once we accept our written questions and answers, we are led to a menu where we can choose five types of different games, namely, matching pairs, word shoot, flashcards, manic miner and cannonball Fun. While if we choose flashcards, questions are presented in that format, if we choose word shoot, answers have to be "shot" once the question is formulated.

An example of an arcade game created by ClassTools is shown in Figure 61.

Figure 61. ClassTools arcade game

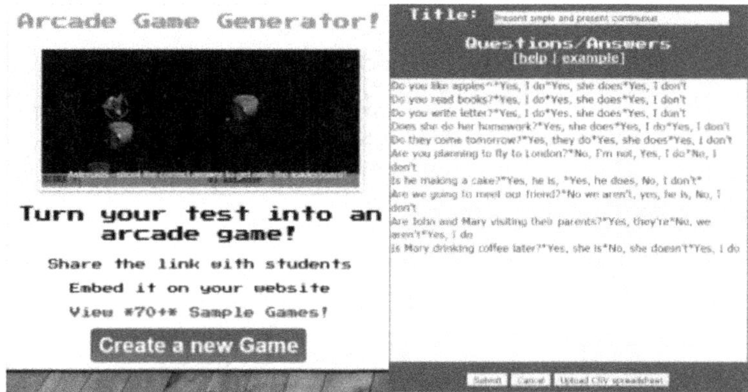

As depicted in Figure 62, ClassTools is also a crossword generator that generates interactive crossword quizzes that can be embedded in websites, blogs or virtual learning platforms. The crosswords can also be exported as a .pdf worksheet.

Figure 62. Crossword generated by ClassTools

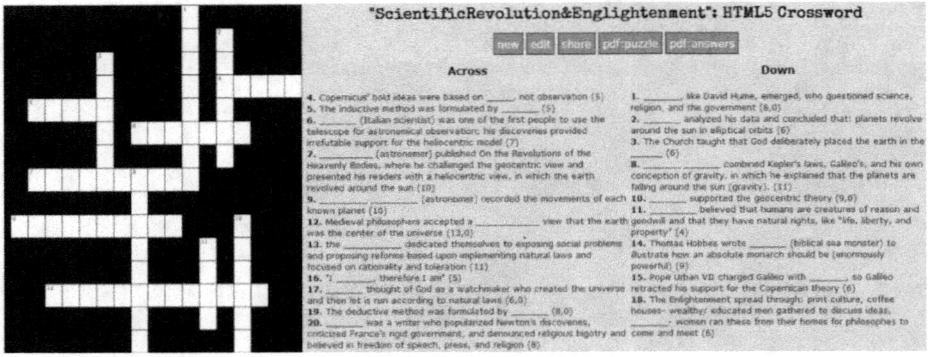

ClassTools also allows to design the so-called Dustbin Game. It is a categorial game through the use of an interface provided by default. A minimum of five words of the same category has to be typed in such as instruments (category)-drums oboe, violin, trumpet and piano. We can use less than four categories. An example of an activity design entails thinking about a main topic debate and decide on four sub-topics per dustbin that will contain more than five debate ideas.

ClassTools is a freely available ICT tool. However, it also gives the option of premium users (20€/year) that allows to have a personal area where all the designed activities can be saved, to show the activities full screen without the presence of ads and bloc ads. Recall that in order to block ads in the free user, we should install AdBlock Plus on Firefox (https://addons.mozilla.org/es-ES/firefox/addon/1865/).

Lingu@net Europa is a metaresource that allows access to other language teaching resources. Searches are done by means of searches in a database of links and the access to the center of resources is multilingual, namely, Dutch, English, French, Italian, German and Spanish. It is useful for teachers, researchers and language learners who can access freely at www.linguanet-worldwide.org/lnetrest/#/selectPublicLanguage/32.

As displayed in Figure 63, three types of searches are available in Lingu@net Europa, namely, textual (dictionaries), categorial (teaching material and original works) and guided (target learning language, student's language, proficiency level, type of didactic content).

Figure 63. Lingu@net

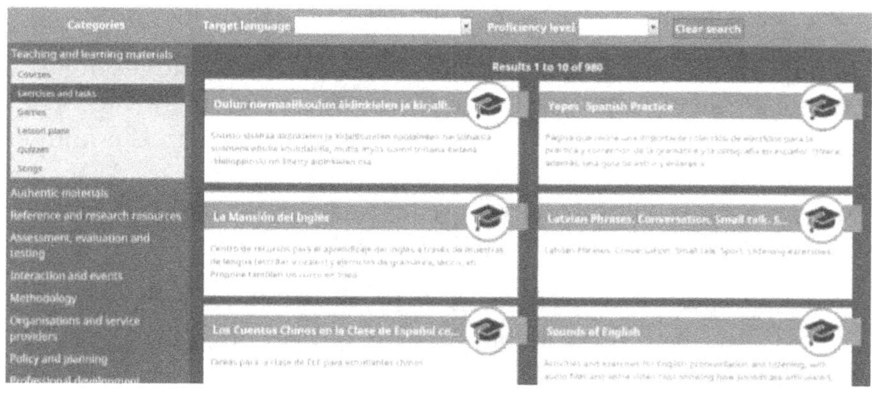

Once the search is done, the user is offered a list of resources that meet the selection criteria requirements. From this list, you can access a file with all the information about the Lingu@net Europa database (for example, access to the virtual Cervantes' center to access resources). Furthermore, Lingu@net offers a consultation service and a distribution list such as Linguaforum that allows to subscribe for free and take part in discussions or receive messages, as available in www.linguanet-worldwide.org/lnetrest/#/forums.

INTEF or the National Institute of Educational Technologies and Teachers' Training belongs to the Spanish Ministry of Education, Culture and Sport. It is responsible for ICT in non-university levels available in https://educalab.es/intef. It offers teaching training resources and a repository of images and audios to be included in teaching design material. INTEF has designed a Samsung Smart School project (https://intef.es/tecnologia-educativa/samsung-smart-school/), coordinated by INTEF and Samsung Spain in collaboration with the autonomous communities. Each school has an ambassador that coordinates the experience of his/her own school to boost the students' learning via mobile phones. Samsung provides teachers and Primary Education students with a tablet. Teachers have to complete an online course, organized by INTEF such as project-based learning, mobile phones and ICT learning.

Educared (http://educared.fundaciontelefonica.com.pe/) belongs to Telefónica Foundation to improve education through ICT tools. It was created in 1998 and offers teaching training courses, teaching material, debates about ICT along with education and society programs.

Childtopia (http://childtopia.com/index.php?module=home) offers English educational games, creativity and artistic designs, photo jigsaws, fun cards, arts and crafts, listen and reading comprehension, classics tales, learning worksheets, and learning to draw tasks.

Agrega project offers free downloadable didactic resources organized in terms of level, topic and subject. It was created by the Spanish Ministry of Education and Science and it is available in the following ULR:
http://agrega2.red.es/visualizadorcontenidos2/Portada/Portada.do;js essionid=8E751C20819B3695D9F45D29D6B9C849.

Learning Space Project is another European library from the Open University of the UK available in http://www.open.edu/openlearn/ about-openlearn /frequently-asked-questions/lookinglearningspace. It offers online didactic resources via online courses that can be downloaded by means of the use of the search bar tool.

Podcasts are a useful tool to develop English speaking comprehension and fluency skills. They enhance the development of different competences, namely, linguistic communication, social and citizenship, learning to learn, autonomy and personal initiative and ICT treatment and digital competence (Nuez García 2010). Podcasts are audio or video files that can be heard or seen directly from a website without the need to download them in the computer. They can also be downloaded automatically in a multimedia player and have been widely used to learn languages to practice oral comprehension. Such is the case of Podcast in English (http://podcastinenglish.com) publishes podcasts regularly with activities. Activities are not designed by the same person; rather, different people intervene, which provides a richer variety of accents and dialects. On the menu, activities are divided into three different levels as well as business English tasks. However, these activities are not free since subscription is 6€ per month. Alternatively, there are a few podcasts (activities and transcriptions are not free) available in http://www.podcastsinenglish.com/pages/freesamples.html.

ESL Pod (www.eslpod.com) and iTunes U (www.apple.com/ education/itunes-u) also host podcasts for L2 English teaching. The latter is part of the iTunes Store and offers free podcasts, conferences, language classes and audiobooks, among others. These podcasts can be played on the iPod, iPhone, Mac or PC.

Listen-to-English (www.listen-to-english.com) is run by the British Council and it offers free access and use of resources. We can subscribe to updates via our email or via RSS. On the menu "archive", we can access 280 podcasts about different topics. The tasks are addressed to intermediate-low level learners because audios are recorded by using a neutral English and at a low pace. Podcasts lasts 3 to 5 minutes.

BBC Podcasts (http://www.bbc.co.uk/podcasts) provide good quality podcasts to learn English as it includes a wide range of speakers. There is free access to resources and the search can be done through the "quick find" or the "genre" options. Nevertheless, there are no transcriptions available in the podcasts. Users can subscribe to updates.

How can we create a podcast? There is a wide range of free programs that allow to record content (music, voice or both) such as Audacity (http://audacity.softonic.com/) and Soundcloud (https://soundcloud.com/). They can be published in a blog, a wiki, a virtual platform or any podcast university such as Ivoox (www.ivoox.com) and Podomatic (www.podomatic.com). There are also websites where podcasts can be uploaded, and they include those ones with a private domain such as Libsyn (www.libsyn.com) and Audioblog (www.audioblog.com) and those ones with a public domain such as Poderato (www.poderato.com) and Podomatic (www.podomatic.com).

The L2 English teaching applications of podcasts entail listening comprehension tasks, students can record themselves and, thus, they play a more active role in using the L2 and in creating dialogues, interviews, radio programs and short videoclips, among others. Podcasts can also be used to work on pronunciation.

## 6. DICTIONARIES AND TRANSLATION PROGRAMS

The dictionary is one of the most relevant sources of linguistic information available (Sevillano García 2009). Teachers should explore the dictionary possibilities as an aid to independent learning. Teachers are required to provide instruction to improve the learners' reference skills.

Examples of English online dictionaries include Webster dictionary (www.m-w.com/dictionary.htm), Linguee (https://linguee.es/), Roget's Internet Thesaurus (www.thesaurus.com), Wordreference (www.wordreference.com), Spanish dictionary (www.spanishdict.com) and All Words (www.allwords.com).

Cambridge University Press (http://dictionary.cambridge.org/dictionary/british/) is an English monolingual dictionary, oral and written pronunciation of words (American, British) and synonyms.

Wordreference (www.wordreference.com) allows to search for the meaning of words and search for translations from language A into language B and vice versa (English, French, Italian, Portuguese, Spanish, among others) as well as definitions and synonyms. In addition, Wordreference includes phonetics, word classes and forum discussions with natives and other speakers in case users are not satisfied with the results obtained.

The University of Granada has designed an idioms dictionary available in http://eubd1.ugr.es/. It allows to translate idioms from English into Spanish and from Spanish into English such as "to kick the bucket" = "*estirar la pata*". Unlike Wordreference, there are no forum discussions.

Other examples of translation dictionaries are listed below:

- Interglot: http://www.interglot.com/dictionary
- Collins: https://www.collinsdictionary.com/translator
- Reverso: http://www.reverso.net/text_translation.aspx?lang=EN
- Cambridge: https://dictionary.cambridge.org/translate/
- Google translate: https://translate.google.com/m/translate
- COBUILD dictionary: www.cobuild.Collins.co.uk/catalogue/cob3flash.html
- Longman Dictionary of Contemporary English: https://www.ldoceonline.com/
- Your dictionary: http://www.yourdictionary.com/

Quizlet (https://quizlet.com/es) allows to create flashcards and exams with different formats such as true/false questions, matching exercises, multiple choice and fill-in the gaps. The main idea of the program is the integration of a word or a question followed by a definition of an answer. The display output changes according to the author's interest. Registration and signing up are required. We can insert the created activities in a blog or virtual learning platforms such as Moodle.

Pro-Profs (www.proprofs.com/quiz-school/) is a free online quiz maker. Quizzes entail questions with multiple choice, true/false, essays, checkbox, fill-in the blank and matching answers. It could be used to make formative and periodic assessments. Furthermore, Pro-Profs (www.proprofs.com/games/) creates the so-called hangman game (access game > hangman > create a hangman game if we want to create one from scratch) or search hangman games (if we want to use one that is already created). If we create a hangman game, register and log in > choose a game name > type in the words that we want to use in the game (each word in a line) > create my game > the program leads us to our created activity. In turn, we can include the created activities in a blog or in an educative platform such as Moodle or Dokeos). Apart from the hangman game, Pro-Profs offers to create other games such as word search, crossword, sliding puzzle and jigsaw puzzles, among others.

Other online teaching resources that allow the creation of activities to be shown in a screen include the Hangman Game (www.hangmanwords.com/create), Click Teaching for Key Stage I and Key Stage II (www.clickteaching.com), Teaching Ideas for Primary Teachers (www.teachingideas.co.uk/subjects/english), Primary Resources (www.primaryresources.co.uk/english/english.htm), Cliparts (www.barrysclipart.com/en/se/clipart), Topmarks for teachers (www.topmarks.co.uk), Hans Andersen's Fairy Tales told online (www.grimmfairytales.com), Fun with Spot with activities to accompany the Spot the Dog books (www.funwithspot.com), Fun Brain (www.funbrain.com/pre-k-and-k-playground), and Grid Club (https://gridclub.com/activities/klik-english).

School Express (www.schoolexpress.com/) enables to design activities related to spelling worksheets, sentences, word unscrambles, word walls and story time tasks. In the case of word ordering activities, click on make word unscrambles > type in the name of the exercise and the list of words that we want the program to show in an unscrambled order (each word in a new line) > submit words > the exercise will be displayed either on the screen or in printed version.

Jigsaw Planet (www.jigsawplanet.com) creates puzzles. Registration and sign in are needed. In order to design a puzzle, click on create > choose an image > decide on the number of puzzle pieces, their shape and if we want them rotated > create. The more difficult the puzzle is, the less focused we are on the content and on the language; thus, it is advisable not to rotate them. For language learners, use letters instead of images to design puzzles. Otherwise, this tool would not have a proper use.

Educima (www.educima.com/crosswordgenerator/spa/) generates crosswords by typing in the title of the crossword, the word to be included and the description or tip so that the student can guess the target word. Finally, click on submit to end the creation process.

## 7. USING ICT TO ANALYZE LANGUAGE VIA CORPUS

A language corpus is a collection of texts that are representative of a language. The body texts are stored in an online database. A language corpus (or language corpora in plural form) can compile written texts or as speech transcribed texts to analyze a particular sound, word or syntactic construction for language study (Crystal 1992).

The British National Corpus (BNC) (https://corpus.bye.edu/bnc/) was originally created by Oxford University Press in the 1980s-early 1990s. It contains 100 million words of written texts from a wide range of genres, namely, spoken, fiction, magazines, newspapers and academic. There is also a search window and you simply type in your phrase into the box and click on search.

For example, if we are searching for the concordance lines for the verbal phrase "have asked". Click on S_meeting to see full context and check the target phrase in the concordance lines in bold. Teachers can copy and paste the results from the search into a word processor to print out for language classroom resources. However, with a very large corpus, there will be material that could be considered unsuitable for some school use.

Figure 64. Concordance line of "have asked" in the BNC

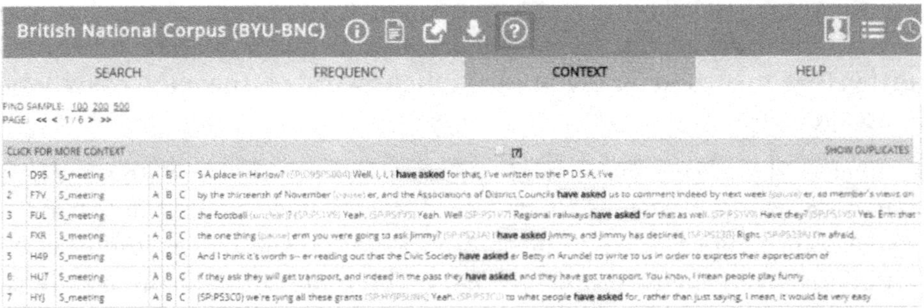

For more sophisticated searches, the use of wildcards is used to see words associated with a phrase. For instance, typing in "happy*" would show you all the words that immediately follow the word happy after the computer has searched the 100 million-word collection of texts. Alternatively, typing in "*happy" would show you all the words that come before the word "happy". You can use more than one wildcard such as "happy**".

The Corpus of Contemporary American English (COCA) is one of the largest available corpus of English and the only large and balanced corpus of American English available in https://corpus.byu.edu/COCA/. It contains more than 560 million words and it is equally divided among spoken, fiction, magazines, newspapers and academic texts.

Chapter **4**

# The use of ICT to communicate and collaborate: The Web 2.0

## 1. THE WEB 2.0: DEFINITION AND MAIN FEATURES

Web 2.0 is also known as social web since it is based on communities of users with common interests that use several services such as blogs, Dropbox, Flickr, podcasts, social networks, wikis and YouTube (Fumero et al. 2007).

Web 1.0 refers to the document-based web, web 2.0 focuses on users and web 3.0 is associated with data (Cobo Romaní and Pardo Kuklinski 2007; Fumero et al. 2007). However, features of the three types of web are found in each of them.

Therefore, web 2.0 moves from conveying information to building knowledge by means of collaborative learning, synchronic and asynchronic learning, new learning competences and new teachers' and learners' roles. Hence, the students in the twenty-first century are known as Einstein's generation, messenger or digital natives (Area Moreira 2009; Bennett 2004).

The term web 2.0 was created by Tim O' Reilly in 2004 and it refers to the second generation of the Internet with new design and use patterns. O' Reilly has described the basic principles of the web 2.0 and are detailed below:

1.  The www is a working platform
2.  The encouragement of collective intelligence
3.  Database management as a basic skill
4.  Models of simple programming and simple searches
5.  Software that is not limited to one single tool
6. The user's positive experiences

Thus, web 2.0 encourages easy and effective exchange of information among users, that is to say, users can create content collaboratively. The services that web 2.0 offers are analogous to big empty shelves and users create, store and distribute their digital devices. This means that users are no longer passive consumers of information; rather, they become active creators of information. Thus, web 2.0 is not a new ICT tool; instead, it is an attitude towards ICT tools in which collaborative work turns into the main features of the actions that are taken on the Internet.

Web 2.0 offers positive opportunities for communication and collaboration and they include access to information, participation in constructing and editing texts, publishing and sharing creative work to a worldwide audience, flexible and dynamic manners of interaction and discussion across a wide range of distances, and varied ways of sharing problem-solving tasks and ideas.

What is the teachers' role in the web 2.0? They can explore new methodological views with new ICT tools and technological resources are required to develop students' learning skills and the curriculum competences. Moreover, teachers must take advantage of the resources that are available to enhance their teaching practices, create shared working school networks and help widespread collaborative work among teachers. In this way, teachers can show their students what good practices are on the Internet and they can create content and multimedia resources. In other words, teachers should guide, advise and evaluate the learning process rather than being the main information source and resources.

The inclusion of ICT tools in schools and universities has permitted a change of the traditional teaching model into a more autonomous, constructive and meaningful learning with higher teaching and pedagogical quality level. In addition, teachers build the working approach to meet the students' varied learning styles and must provide a wide range of evaluation procedures such as self-correction and written feedback.

The teacher must support students in the completion of ICT tasks, select the appropriate ICT tools according to the aims, contents and basic abilities of the educational modules. Therefore, teachers have to (a) motivate and guide students; (b) select and organize the teaching content; (c) generate learning resources; and (d) facilitate and evaluate the students' learning process.

A summary of the features that underlie web 1.0, web 2.0 and web 3.0 is depicted in Table 6.

Table 6. Web 1.0, web 2.0 and web 3.0

| Web 1.0 (1993-2003) | Web 2.0 (2004-2012) | Web 3.0 (ongoing) |
|---|---|---|
| Many websites to be visited through a browser | Many shared content through highly interactive services | Information that is already published is organized and made accessible for users |
| Reading (users) | Shared reading | For example, conceptual maps where all the available online information is related to give answers to a particular question |
| Editors (webmasters)-reception | We are all editors-production | |
| Static and unidirectional | Dynamic and multidirectional (user's participation) | |

Web 1.0 and web 2.0 mainly differ in the way the content is managed and the type of the user's intervention. In web 2.0, the content can be managed by the person that generates the website and by the users who can participate in creating, organizing and sharing the content. Therefore, from web 1.0 to web 2.0, we go from an approach in which the information transferred is crucial given that users are information receives to an approach in which sharing information is relevant since users are receivers and senders.

Cobo and Pardo (2007) suggest for types of learning in the web 2.0: (a) learning by doing via a process of individual and collective creation where a constructive learning approach is promoted; (b) learning by interacting by means of exchanging ideas with other Internet users; (c) learning by searching by means of a process of investigation, selection and adjustment that ends up by enriching of the user that develops these skills; and (d) learning by sharing.

Table 7 illustrates a description of the language teachers' competences per language skill associated with what ICT resources are effective in the development of each skill (reading, writing, listening and speaking).

Table 7. ICT resources per language skill

| Skill | Language teachers' competences | ICT resources |
|---|---|---|
| Reading | -To encourage students digital reading, searching for texts on the Internet<br>-To design digital reading worksheets from what has been read and share them<br>-To know the main resources related to digital reading: tools, platforms, forums and chats | -Digital libraries/online newspapers (http://kiosko.net/)<br>-Repositories or programs to share data on the cloud (creation of shared reading worksheets)<br>-Forums and chats focused on a reading topic<br>-Search for texts in different digital devices (smartphones, tablets, etc.)<br>-Knowledge and use of digital reading formats (http://www.starfall.com/index.htm<br>-Creation of virtual characters with voice (http://www.voki.com/) |
| Writing | -To know the main programs to write digitally: Word processors, editing programs (blogs, wikis, etc.)<br>-To adjust writing to the digital device/format | -Blogs and wikis (http://www.zinepal.com/) (they generate magazines from blogs)<br>-Word processors<br>-Social blogging programs (Twitter, Edmodo, Facebook, etc.)<br>-Instant messaging programs (WhatsApp, Line, etc.)<br>-Super stickers (http://wigflip.com/superstickies/) |
| Listening | -To use devices and audio editing programs to encourage listening comprehension<br>-To search for original audio material and to know how to download it and adjust it to the aim of the task (phonetics, rhythm, intonation) | -Podcasts, YouTube or related<br>-Streaming (a tiempo real)<br>-Songs: http://www.angles365.com/classroom/songsci03.htm -Conversor from text to mp3: http://vozme.com/index.php?Lang=es<br>-Audio cutter (http://cut-mp3.com/es/) Audio joiner (http://audio-joiner.com/es/)<br>-Creation of presentations with music from pictures (http://animoto.com/; www.prezi.com) |
| Speaking | -To know the use of recording programs to widespread on the Internet<br>-To know synthesizing programs from written to oral format | -Audio recording programs (CoolEdit, Audacity, Nero wave, etc.)<br>-Synthesizing programs (Loquendo/Vozme/YAKiToMe)<br>-Vocabulary learning: http://concurso.cnice.mec.es/cnice2005/132_English_for_Little_children/presentacion/present ac ion.html<br>-Creation of digital cartoons (http://www.xtranormal.com/)<br>-Adding voice/sound to images/cartoons (www.voki.com; https://blabberize.com/)<br>-Provide subtitles to YouTube videos (www.amara.org/es)<br>-Record and distribute conferences/presentations: CAMTASIA RELAY (http://www.techsmith.com/camtasia-relay.html) |

## 2. THE WEB 2.0: TOOLS AND APPLICATIONS

The web 2.0 offers a wide range of tools and applications such as social networking sites, blogs, google drive, wikis, digital books, podcasts, Moodle, word clouds and social repositories.

Social networking sites aim to ease users' communication with colleagues, friends and other people with shared interests. Such is the example of Facebook, twitter, LinkedIn or google+. There are other informal language learning platforms such as busuu (www.busuu.com) that provides free resources for learning any language and offers contact with native speakers.

Blogs are the main format of publication in the web 2.0. They aim to transfer information and interaction with other users by means of the use of comments. Etymologically, the term weblog was coined by Barger in 1977. The short version (that is, blog) was coined by Merholz who divided the word weblog in the phrase "we blog" in 1999. Blogger is the person that writes and edits blogs.

Blogs offer service of publishing and sharing content. Indeed, they started as personal diaries in which users wrote about their insights and experiences. They also allow the chance to develop communicative skills in a written format in the L1 and in the L2. Readers can subscribe to blogs for free via RSS (Really Simple Syndication) that allows to receive updates of blogs that we are interested in. The content in blogs is chronologically presented; however, the blog publication does not have to be daily although it will be highly valued if the content is frequently published and shared. In addition, readers can communicate with the author via comments and suggestions associated with the content discussed. An example of a classroom blog that also includes students' bogs is available in http://cuartode.wordpress.com/.

Blogs can include gadgets and widgets. They refer to small applications or programs that permit access to functions and display visual information. Examples of gadgets and widgets involve calendars, clocks, list of links, images and the weather. We can also block undesired people's comments, list the last added comments by readers, retrieve statistics of visits and trackback, that is, an automatic notification when another blog has linked some of the articles. These applications usually appear in the side bars of blogs.

Blogs can contribute to teaching and learning since they boost writing, enable instantaneous publication on the Internet, combine content, pictures and links. In the case of L2 English teaching, blogs offer students the means of publication for work that may otherwise have been restricted to exercise books. Furthermore, they offer high potential audience, namely, the teacher, the class and expanded worldwide. Indeed, the audience can answer instantly.

Blogs can be created by using blogger (http://www.blogger.com) and a Gmail account is needed. Click on "create a blog" (top right corner button), give a title to your blog, choose the first part of the URL for your blog. Then, choose a short and easy name to remember. The second part is blogspot.com that cannot be changed (for instance, http://secondamusic.blogspot.com). Click on "check availability" because if the URL has been previously created, it needs to be changed. Type in the letters that you see in the image and click on "continue". You are led to a screen in which you have to decide the style of your blog and click on "start publishing". You can change the appearance of the blog > type in your article > insert images/videos. Pay attention to "entry tags", namely, words that describe the content of the article so that it can be easily found on the Internet. Finally, click on "publish entry".

We can also create blogs with blogetery (http://blogetery.com/), google sites (https://sites.google.com/?hl=es), Weebly (http://www.weebly.com/index.php?Lang=es) and Tumblr (www.tumblr.com).

In order to make a blog more attractive, we can use Google Analytics (https://analytics.google.com/analytics/web/provision/?authuser=0#provision/SignUp/), Only Wire to connect a blog to more than 50 social networks (https://www.onlywire.com/), Chat Wing to create a chat window so that users can communicate live (https://chatwing.com/), FSCapture to capture and annotate any element on the screen (http://www.faststone.org/FSCaptureDetail.htm), Free Mind to create schemas (https://freemind.softonic.com/), MindMesiter to create conceptual maps (https://wwwmindmesiter.com/es), and Pixton to design comics (https://www.pixton.com/es/).

Here is a list of blogs for L2 English learning and teaching:

- ICT blog in foreign languages:
  Recursostic.educación.es/blogs/malted/index.php/2012/03/03/del-grupo-dedebate-al-podcast
- Aula21 blog: www.aula21.net/aulablog21
- My place for English: http://myplaceforenglish.blogspot.com/

Google Drive is a free online office site available in https://www.google.com/intl/es_ALL/drive/. Users can write and edit their documents from anywhere if they have access to the Internet. It also allows groups of members to collaborate on the elaboration of a text at the same time.

Wikis refer to websites that can be edited by users. Thus, it is a collective writing ICT tool, it enhances collaborative work and success will depend on the users' contributions given that they are the ones that create, keep and improve the wikis. Learners can generate resources collectively so that other peers can see the results instantly. More specifically, a wiki page is a blank page. The project could show information based on a topic or on specific resources. There is often a discussion facility that enhances students to comment on the content.

Wikis can be created through the use of WordPress (http://wordpres.org), Vox (www.vox.com), Blogger (www.blogger.com) and Wikispaces (www.wikispaces.com).

Examples of free online wikis include the following ones:

1. Wikipedia: http://es.wikipedia.org/wiki/wikimedia
2. Wikispaces: www.wikispaces.com (it offers the option to create a free wiki if you justify affiliation to a school)
3. Wikidictionary: meaning of words, synonyms, etymology, translations
4. Wikibooks
5. Wikisource: original works
6. Wikiquote: famous quotes
7. Wikimedia Commons: images, audios and videos
8. Wikinews

Lesson plans can revolve around a wiki project such as newspapers or school magazines, glossaries, dictionaries, encyclopedias, research projects, topic-based or thematic wikis. Examples of the latter include Gleducar wiki based on the use of ICT tools in Argentinian schools (http://wiki.gleducar.org.ar/), WikiDidaTICa, an ICT oriented project (http://recursostic.educación.es/multidisciplinar/wikididactica/index .php), let's TIC English (https://letsticenglish.wikispaces.com/), EFL and Web 2.0 (http://eflcourse.wikispaces.com/) and English Society and Culture (http://englishsocietyandculture.wikispaces.com/).

ICT tools to communicate and collaborate in the web 2.0 is the creation of digital books with Flipsnack (www.flipsnack.com/es/). This tool allows to convert a .pdf format into a digital .html book format. The platform requires users to register and sign in. One of the potentials of Flipsnack is that L2 English teachers can ask students to write an essay in Microsoft Word format. The first page should be the cover, the second page should be the table of contents and the subsequent pages should have the content (one page is one piece of content that will later be published and shared among their peers). Save the Microsoft Word file as a .pdf. Then, sign in Flipsnack, upload your pdf and customize the appearance of your publication. Finally, copy the embedded link (you can send it to other users via email or other means).

Therefore, digital books will encourage L2 English learners' motivation to develop their writing skills, they can be read by a large audience rather than mainly being read by the teacher and the format is more attractive when compared to that of blogs.

An example of a digital book is shown in Figure 64, created by the Secondary School Cavaleri to collect all the students' pieces of writings during the academic course 2008-2009 associated with all the modules they were enrolled in. It is available in http://iescavaleri.com/my2008.

Figure 64. Digital book

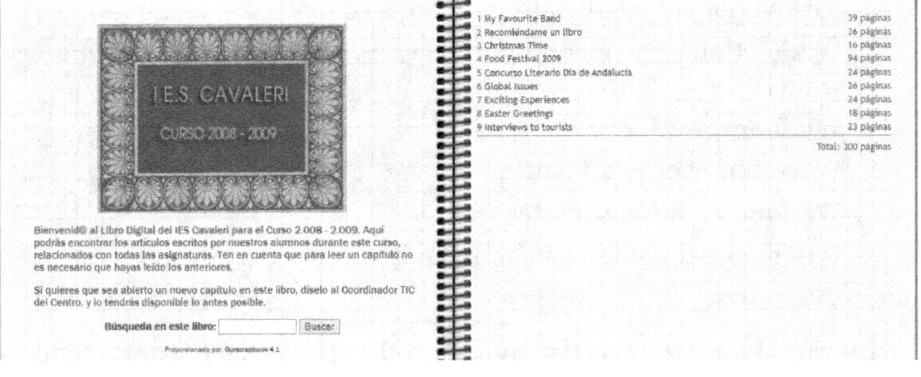



Moodle stands for Modular Object-Oriented Dynamic Learning Environment. It was created by Martin Dougiamas in the 1960s and its main moto is constructive learning. Moodle allows L2 English teachers to exploit the pedagogical use of the Internet through the implementation of seven modules, namely, task, consultation, forum, questionnaire, resource, survey and workshop. In the task module, teachers can arrange deadlines and the highest score that can be given to students; students' tasks can be uploaded, and the uploading date is registered; finally, feedback is provided. The consultation module can be used to vote for something or receive an answer from each student.

The forum module includes topics of discussion. The questionnaire module consists of multiple-choice questions, short answers, true and false tests and cloze tests. The resource module implies files that can be uploaded in any format such as word, power point, Prezi, video or sound. The survey module is used to analyze how the classes went and reports are available; graphs and results can be displayed in Excel or in CVS format. The workshop module allows the assessment of documents among students and the teacher can manage and evaluate the assessment.

Word clouds are useful to learn vocabulary and to motivate students towards a specific topic. L2 English teachers can display a brainstorming of ideas and work with word classifications such as synonyms and verbs. The tool that generates word clouds is Wordle (www.wordle.net). In order to create the word cloud in Figure 65, we click on the create button, type in the words we want students to learn and leaving a space between them and, finally, click on the go button.

Figure 65. Word cloud

If you include several repeated words on Wordle, they will appear more frequently on the cloud. The randomized button will make the appearance of the word cloud change every time it is clicked. We can also edit the language, the font, the layout and the color. When we save the Wordle file, an URL is generated, and you can use it in any other circumstances.

Word clouds can be used in the L2 English classroom for memory games. The teacher will ask the students to search for words related to a topic. The teacher (or a student) will write them on the introductory slot of the program. Students are given 30 to 60 seconds to memorize all the words that they can. Then, the screen is turned off and the students are asked to write as many words as they can remember.

Another teaching and learning word cloud activity is the creation of a long sentence. In pairs or in groups, students have to create a logical sentence by using as many words as they can in the Wordle (in this case, the screen is not turned off). Naturally, they can use other words apart from the Wordle ones.

Poster design can be carried out with the ICT tool Automotivator (http://wigflip.com/automotivator/). The program does not require registration and the design of posters will include a picture, a short text (a famous phrase, a motivating phrase, a motto or a book title). The poster has a .jpg format that we can print or save in our computers to include it in a blog, a social network or Flickr. The interface allows users to select a random image from their computers or a website; once users have clicked on "go", they are asked to type in the title and the font (only two fonts are allowed). In the second window of the interface, users will be required to write the subtitle and the poster is done (see the preview).

Glogster (www.gogster.com) is a free website that allows the design of more elaborated online multimedia posters. We need to register before using it. Posters are created and self-published on the Internet. They show texts, pictures, sounds, videos and links to other websites. The application allows to send emails to other users, check the number of followers and check the number of visits and the score they have given to the poster. We can include the poster in our blog and send it by email or via social networks.

Considering the terminology related to Glogster, the eduglog refers to the educational glog; glogger is the glog's author; and glogosfera is the collection of glogs published on the Internet. Indeed, Glogster allows to publish posters privately or publicly and record (with a microphone and a webcam) audio and video from the program. It also displays a wide range of tools such as frames for images, bubbles and objects, among others.

An example of a poster designed by Glogster is illustrated in Figure 66.

Figure 66. Poster created by Glogster

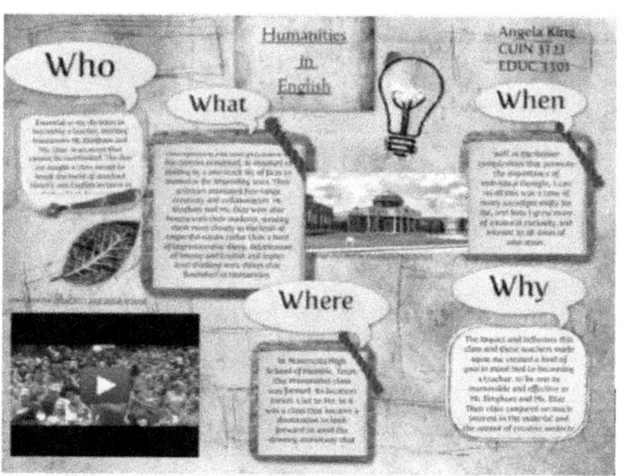


Social repositories refer to a collection of resources added by users with the aim of sharing them. They have the capacity to communicate with other users and are useful to comment, vote and tag other users. Examples of social repositories include those ones that revolve around images such as Flickr (www.flickr.com) and videos such as YouTube (www.youtube.com). The YouTube educative variant that filters pedagogical videos is available in www.teachertube.com or www.youtube.com/education. Other social repositories entail documents such as Scribd (www.scribd.com) and presentations such as Slideshare (www.slideshare.com).

# References

Adell, J. (2004). "Internet en el aula: las Webquest." *Edutec Revista Electrónica de Tecnología Educativa* 17, a036. https://doi.org/10.21556/edutec.2004.17.530

Ambròs Pallarès, A. and Breu Pañella, R. (2007). *Cine y Educación: el Cine en el Aula de Primaria y Secundaria*. Barcelona: Ed. Graó.

Anderson, J. and Van Weert, T. (2002). *Information and Communication Technology in Education: A Curriculum for Schools and Programme of Teacher Development*. Francia: Division of Higher Education.

Area Moreira, M. (2009). *Introducción a la Tecnología Educativa*. La Laguna: Universidad.

Barba Coromines, C., Capella Priu, S., Adell Segura, J. and Dodge, B. (2010). Ordenadores en las aulas. Barcelona: Ed. Graó.

Barberá, E. (2004). *La Educación en la Red: Actividades Virtuales de Enseñanza y Aprendizaje*. Barcelona/Buenos Aires/México: Paidós.

Barberà, E. and Badia, A. (2004). *Educar con Aulas Virtuales: Orientaciones para la Innovación en el Proceso de Enseñanza y Aprendizaje*. Madrid: A. Machado.

Bennett, R. (2004). *Using ICT in Primary English Teaching*. New York: Learning Matters.

Bernat, A. and Gros, B. (2008). *Videojuegos y Aprendizaje*. Barcelona: Graó.

Blanco, R. and Cervera, D. (2010). *Tecnología: Investigación, Innovación y Buenas Prácticas*. Madrid-Barcelona: MEC- Ed. Graó.

Cabero Almenara, J. (Coord.) (2006). *Nuevas Tecnologías Aplicadas a la Educación*. Madrid: McGraw Hill.

Cabero Almenara, J. (Coord.) (2007). *Tecnología Educativa*. Madrid: McGraw Hill.

Cabero Almenara, J. and Román Graván, P. (Coords.). (2008). *E-actividades*. Alcalá de Guadaira, Sevilla: MAD.

Castañeda Quintero, L. (2010). *Aprendizaje con Redes Sociales: Tejidos Educativos para los Nuevos Entornos*. Alcalá de Guadaira, Sevilla: MAD.

Castro Sánchez, J. J. (2004). *Las Tecnologías de la Información y Comunicación (TIC) como Apoyo a la Enseñanza Presencial en la Universidad de las Palmas de Gran Canaria*. Las Palmas de Gran Canaria: Universidad de las Palmas de Gran Canaria, Vicerrectorado de Planificación y Calidad.

Cervera, D. and Blanco, R. (2010). *Didáctica de la Tecnología*. Barcelona: Ed. Graó.

Cobo Romaní, C. and Pardo Kuklinski, H. (2007). *Planeta Web 2.0: Inteligencia Colectiva o Medios Fast Food*. Barcelona/México DF: Grup de Recerca D' Interaccions Digitals, Universitat de Vic. Flacso México.

Commission of the European Communities (2001). *Communication from the Commission to the Council and the European Parliament: The eLearning Action Plan. Designing Tomorrow's Education.* Available in https://eur-lex.europa.eu/LexUriServ/LexUriServ.do?uri=COM:2001:0172:FIN:EN:PDF

Crystal, David. 1992. An Encyclopedic Dictionary of Language and Languages. Oxford: Blackwell.

Cukierman, U., Rozenhauz, J. and Santángelo, H. (2009). *Tecnología Educativa.* Buenos Aires: Prentice HallPearson.

De Benito Crosetti, B. and Salinas Ibáñez, J. (2016). "La Investigación Basada en Diseño en Tecnología Educativa". *Revista Interuniversitaria de Investigación en Tecnología Educativa* 0: 44-59.

De la Cruz Cabanillas, I. and Tejedor Martínez, C. (2003). *La Aplicación de las Nuevas Tecnologías al Aprendizaje y Enseñanza de Lengua Inglesa.* Universidad de Alcalá: Colección Aula Abierta.

Díaz de Prado, F. and Cervera, D. (2010). *Tecnología: Complementos de Formación Disciplinar.* Madrid-Barcelona: MEC- Ed. Graó.

Escudero, J. (1995). "La Integración de las Nuevas Tecnologías en el Curriculum y en el Sistema Escolar." In Rodríguez Dieguez, J. L. and Sáez Barrio, O. (eds). *Tecnología Educativa. Nuevas Tecnologías Aplicadas a la Educación.* Alcoy: Marfil.

European Computer Driving License Guide. Available in http://ecdl.cc.uah.es/G.pdf.

Fonoll Salvador, J., García Fernández, J., García Villalobos, J., Guerra Álvarez, A., Gutiérrez and Restrepo, E., Jaúdenes Casaubón, C., Martínez Normand, L., and Romero Zúnica, R. (2011). *Accesibilidad, TIC y Educación.* Madrid: Ministerio de Educación.

Fumero, A., Roca, G. and Sáez Vacas, F. (2007). *Web 2.0.* Madrid: Fundación Orange.

Gallego, D. J. and Gatica, N. (Coords.). (2010). *La Pizarra Digital.* Alcalá de Guadaira, Sevilla: MAD.

García-Valcárcel Muñoz-Repiso, A. and Hernández Martín, A. (2013). *Recursos Tecnológicos para la Enseñanza e Innovación Educativa.* Madrid: Síntesis.

Gimeno Sanz, A. M. (2002). *Tecnologías de la Información y de las Comunicaciones en la Enseñanza de ELE.* Valencia: Universidad Politécnica de Valencia.

Gargallo López, B. and Suárez Rodríguez, J. (2003). *La Integración de las Nuevas Tecnologías en los Centros.* Madrid: Secretaría General Técnica.

Kleinrock, L. (1961). *Information Flow in Large Communication Nets.* PhD dissertation, MIT

Martínez Sánchez, F. and Prendes Espinosa, M. P. (Coords) (2008). *Nuevas Tecnologías y Educación.* Madrid: Pearson.

Manning, C. D., Raghavan, P. and Schütze, H. (2008). *Introduction to Information Retrieval.* Cambridge: Cambridge University Press.

Nuez García, C. L. (2010). "El Podcast: un Recurso Didáctico para el Aula de Música." *El Guiniguada*: 97-110.

O'Reilly, Tim, "What Is Web 2.0. Design Patterns and Business Models for the Next Generation of Software", available in http://www.oreillynet.com/pub/a/oreilly/tim/news/2005/09/30/what-is-web-20.html

Pereira Domínguez, C. (2005). *Los Valores del Cine de Animación: Propuestas Pedagógicas para Padres y Educadores*. Barcelona: PPU.

Porrás, P. and Salaar, J. (2002). "Internet: Comunicación, Información y Servicios." In P. Porrás and J. Salazar (Eds.). *La Discapacidad en Internet* (pp. 17-21). Minusval.

Rank, T., Millum, T. and Warren, C. (2011*). Teaching English Using ICT: A Practical Guide for Secondary School Teachers*. London: A&C Black.

Reyzábal Manso, M. I. and Santiuste Bermejo, V. (2006). *Lenguaje y Nuevas Tecnologías: de la Gramática Generativa a la Tecnología del Habla*. Madrid: CCS.

Rodriguez Terceño, J. (2012). *Aplicaciones del EEES a partir de la Web 2.0 y 3.0*. Madrid: Visión Libros.

Ruiz Dávila, M., Montero Pascual, E. and Díaz Tejero, B. (2010). *Aprendiendo con Videojuegos: Jugar es Pensar Dos Veces*. Madrid: Narcea.

Salazar Noguera, J. and Juan Garau, M. (2009). *Aprendizaje Integrado de Lengua Inglesa y Contenidos Multiculturales*. Barcelona: Edicions UIB.

Sánchez Rodríguez, J., Ruíz Palmero, J. and Palomo López, R. (2008). *Enseñanza con TIC en el Siglo XXI: la Escuela 2.0*. Alcalá de Guadaira, Sevilla: MAD.

Sardelich, M. E. (2006). *Las Nuevas Tecnologías en Educación*. Vigo: Ideaspropias.

Segovia García, N. (2006). *Aplicación de las TIC's a la Docencia*. Vigo: Ideaspropias.

Sevillano García, M. L. (2009). *Competencias para el Uso de Herramientas Virtuales en la Vida, Trabajo y Formación Permanentes*. Madrid: Prentice Hall- Pearson.

Sevillano García, M. L. and Fernández Muñoz, R. (2002). *Nuevas Tecnologías, Medios de Comunicación y Educación*. Madrid: CCS.

Silva Salinas, S. (2005). *Medios Didácticos Multimedia para el Aula*. Vigo: Ideaspropias.

Souto Moure, A. (2006). *Formador de Teleformadores*. Vigo: Ideaspropias.

State Royal Decree 1513/2006, 7 December. (BOE 5, 8th December 2006).

State Royal Decree 1631/2006, 29th December. (BOE 5, 5th January 2007).

Temprano Sánchez, A. (2011). *Las TIC en la Enseñanza Bilingüe. Recursos Prácticos para la Creación de Actividades Interactivas y Motivadoras*. Alcalá de Guadaira, Sevilla: MAD.

Toledo, P. (2013). "Las Tecnologías de la Información, la Comunicación y la Inclusión Educativa." In J. Barroso and J. Cabero (Eds.). *Nuevos Escenarios Digitales* (441-426). Madrid: Pirámide.

Toledo Morales, P. and Hervás Gómez, C. (2009). *El Software Libre en los Contextos Educativos*. Alcalá de Guadaira, Sevilla: MAD.

Vivancos Martí, J. (2008). *Tratamiento de la Información y Competencia Digital*. Madrid: Alianza.